D0852753

The Dirt Doctor's Guide to Organic Gardening

Essays on the Natural Way

J. HOWARD GARRETT

The Dirt Doctor's Guide to Organic Gardening

UNIVERSITY OF TEXAS PRESS
AUSTIN

First edition, 1995

Requests for permission to reproduce material
from this work should be sent to
Permissions, University of Texas Press,
Box 7819, Austin, TX 78713-7819.

⊗ The paper used in this publication meets the
minimum requirements of American National Standard
for Information Sciences—Permanence of Paper
for Printed Library Materials, ANSI Z39.48-1984.

LIBRARY OF CONGRESS
CATALOGING-IN-PUBLICATION DATA

Garrett, Howard, 1947–
The dirt doctor's guide to organic gardening : essays on the
natural way / J. Howard Garrett. — 1st ed.
        p.   cm.
    Includes index.
    ISBN 0-292-72780-1. — ISBN 0-292-72781-x (pbk.)
    1. Organic gardening.   2. Organic gardening—Texas.
    I. Title.
SB453.5.G36   1995
635′.0484—dc20   95-1488

To My Critics

Without their unintentional help,
I would not have researched,
studied, and worked as hard
as I have to better understand nature
and help communicate its secrets to others.

Contents

Acknowledgments

Thanks to the *Dallas Morning News,* especially editors Bob Bersano and Martha Sheridan, for using my organic information in the House and Garden section of the paper. Many of these essays appeared in one form or another in my weekly column. Many thanks also to Donna Wilkins and Tracy Flanagan, my assistants. Both worked many hours typing, editing, revising, and helping to keep me on track.

Introduction

Organics is controversial. Organiphobes still exist today and they want organics to fail. The pressures are great from chemical companies, people who make their living recommending chemicals, advertisers with truckloads of money, and people who simply don't understand what we are talking about. I hope this book will uncover some of those issues while at the same time explaining in detail how easy it is to be successful using organic techniques.

An organic landscape maintenance program is not primarily about which pesticides to use. Its goal is to eliminate pesticides completely. While that is a lofty long-term goal, the organic program uses the lowest-toxicity pesticides possible and, when available, those that are biological and harmful only to the targeted pest. A true organic program is an entirely different philosophy and attitude. Traditional chemical programs are built around a "force-feeding" philosophy of plant fertility and a "kill" philosophy of pest control. A truly organic program, on the other hand, is built around a "health" philosophy and has the primary goal of establishing a natural balance of soil, water, air, and biology. Looked at in the simplest terms, an organic program increases the air and the organic matter in the soil, uses naturally balanced fertilizers, keeps all bare soil mulched, and increases soil life and insect life. Healthy soil produces healthy plants that have very powerful resistance to insects and diseases. Organic pesticides are used, but only as a last resort; whenever possible, beneficial insects are used instead, and if the rest of the program is done correctly, the pesticides are rarely if ever needed.

This book is a compilation of revised versions of some of my past columns, stories, articles, speeches, and thoughts on what I call "The Natural Way." Although some of these essays are similar to past *Dallas Morning News* columns and stories I wrote for various magazines, there are two main differences. These essays are more harshly to the point than my original writings were, and they have all been rewritten to be clearer, more accurate, and more up to date. I know more now than I did when I wrote the original versions. I learn something new every day. It would frustrate some people to tears, but I love to learn new things—new concepts, new science and new techniques—and when I learn that I've been wrong, I'm delighted to be the first to admit it and pass along the new information. I'm not afraid to admit being wrong. In the past I recommended the use of gypsum on all soils, instead of just those deficient in sulfur and calcium, as I recommend now. In the past I recommended spraying soaps regularly; I don't recommend soaps much at all anymore. I know now that they are harmful to soil life if overused. I don't recommend organic pesticides nearly as much anymore, either—except as a last resort. I now advise gardeners to spray once if needed and to stop the use as soon as possible. I recommend different soil testing than I did before, and tomorrow I may make some other changes; in fact, I'm sure I will.

Although the picture is starting to change now, organic gardeners don't have as much support from land grant universities as the chemical people do. We have to learn from the real "old-timers" and increase our knowledge as we go along—often by trial and error. However, our way is, itself, pure science. It is the integration of chemistry, physics, and biology. This holistic, scientific approach has a name—not a new name—simply one that has been ignored by those specializing in limited areas. It's called The Natural Way.

The Dirt Doctor's Guide to Organic Gardening

1 Basics of Organics

Where Do I Start?

Over the years I've been asked lots of questions about organics. Some are asked often. The most common question comes in various forms, but asks the same thing: *I'm ready. The chemical approach isn't working and I'm ready. The only problem is, I don't understand how to start. What do I do first?* Okay, here we go. Any new thought process or activity seems complicated at first, but this one really is quite simple. Here's how The Natural Way works.

ORGANIC CONCEPTS

Step 1. Stop using artificial pesticides and artificial fertilizers. Artificial products feed the plants in an unbalanced way, and pesticides don't control pests in the long term.

Step 2. Increase air in the soil through mechanical aeration. Punch holes in the ground. Deep penetration and ripping with power tools is the most effective technique.

Step 3. Increase the organic matter in the soil. Use compost and 100-percent-organic fertilizers to feed the soil. Let the fertile soil feed the plants.

Step 4. Add rock powders to increase trace minerals. The best materials are those from volcanic activity, such as granite, lava sand, and zeolite. Also effective are greensand, colloidal phosphate (also called soft rock phosphate), and glacial rock powder.

Step 5. Cover all bare soil around plants with natural mulch. Avoid artificial mulches or plastic materials.

Step 6. Encourage life and biodiversity by introducing beneficial insects and protecting those that already exist. Buy ladybugs, green lacewings, and trichogramma wasps. You'll need to buy fewer every year because natural populations will establish.

Step 7. Select native or adapted plants; otherwise, the first six points don't matter. Good soil and perfect fertility will never make date palms grow well in Dallas, but if wise plant choices are made, the organic program will work beautifully.

Step 8. Spray to kill—not! The organic spray program applies materials that stimulate life and health. Foliar feeding is a very efficient way to give plants organic matter and micronutrients. Use a mixture of fish emulsion, liquid seaweed, and molasses as a base. I'll explain how to supplement this mixture to correct specific deficiencies.

Step 9. Encourage biodiversity. Introduce and maintain a wide variety of plant species. Use natives and well-adapted plants from other regions. Nature doesn't allow monocultures, so why should we? If you follow all of these steps, additional biodiversity will materialize like magic. Birds and other friends such as bats, lizards, toads, and beneficial insects will take up residence.

The secret is understanding that we human types are part of nature—not in control of it. It's all about life, balance, and common sense. No program but nature's is perfect. Mine is no exception, and I suggest that you start with it and massage it through trial and error until the best formula for you becomes evident. One of the most pleasant aspects of organic landscaping and gardening is the forgiving tolerance of healthy soil and adapted plants; they have tremendous buffering powers to help us feeble gardeners. If we establish the right conditions, nature will perfect our gardens, lawns, farms, and ranches for us by bringing all the elements into balance.

Basic Organic Program

Some years ago, I started writing a short explanation on how to carry out an organic program. It has since been edited, revised, and expanded many times. Here's the current version:

Soil testing. Have soil tested, by a lab that gives organic recommendations, to learn the total and available levels of organic matter, nitrogen, calcium, magnesium, sulfur, phosphates, potassium, sodium, chloride, boron, iron, manganese, copper, and zinc. Check for life by counting the earthworms in a square foot of soil—there should be at least ten.

Aerating. Mechanically aerate soil so that drainage is improved, microbes are stimulated, and tied-up nutrients are released. The best tools are those that puncture and tear or rip the soil. A 2-inch depth is beneficial, though 6 or 7 inches is better.

Planting. Prepare new planting beds by scraping away existing grass and weeds, adding 4–6 inches of compost, and tilling 3 inches into the native soil. Good additional ingredients include rock powders such as granite sand, greensand, lava sand, zeolite, or colloidal phosphate at 40–80 pounds per 1,000 square feet and organic fertilizer at 20 pounds per 1,000 square feet. Do not use raw bark, peat moss, concrete sand, or artificial fertilizers.

Fertilizing. Apply 100-percent-natural organic fertilizer to all turf and planting areas in early spring, at 10–20 pounds per 1,000 square feet. Repeat every 60 to 90 days during the growing season if phosphorus and potassium levels remain low. Apply rock powder annually, at about 10–40 pounds per 1,000 square feet. The best choices include lava sand, granite dust, zeolite, and other volcanic materials. Add bat guano, fish meal, kelp meal, or earthworm castings, at 10–20 pounds per 1,000 square feet, to annuals and perennials in the spring and, if phosphorus and potassium are low, every 60–90 days during the growing season. Add a small handful of earthworm castings or colloidal phosphate to each hole when planting bulbs or small transplants. Mist or soak bulbs or seeds before planting in a 1 percent solution of seaweed or other biostimulant.

Foliar feeding. Foliar feed all plants with a liquid mixture of fish emulsion, seaweed, natural apple cider vinegar, and blackstrap molasses, all at 1 tablespoon per gallon of water. For iron deficiency, add chelated iron and Epsom salts, at 1 tablespoon per gallon.

Mulching. Nature doesn't allow bare soil and neither should we. Mulch preserves moisture, eliminates weeds, and keeps the soil surface cooler, which benefits earthworms and microorganisms. For shrubs, trees, and groundcovers, use at least 1 inch of compost and 3 inches of shredded native wood chips or shredded hardwood bark. Mulch vegetable gardens with 8 inches of wheat straw or, better still, alfalfa hay. Partially completed compost is also an excellent topdressing.

Mowing/trimming. Mow higher than the organiphobes recommend. Do not scalp the lawn in the spring—start the season at no lower than 2 inches and raise to at least 3 inches by midsummer. Mow weekly or more often if necessary, leaving the clippings on the lawn. Put occasional excess clippings in the compost pile. Do not send bagged clippings to the dump. Do not use weed eaters around trees.

Watering. Adjust schedule seasonally to allow for deep, infrequent waterings in order to maintain an even moisture level. About 1 inch of water per week in the summer is a good starting point. When possible, add 1 tablespoon of natural apple cider vinegar per gallon of water. Use a siphon attachment and include a light application of fish emulsion and seaweed when possible, too.

Weeding. Pull large weeds by hand, mulch all bare soil, and work on soil health for overall control. AVOID CHEMICAL HERBICIDES, especially pre-emergent types and those that contain 2, 4-D, which is a broadleaf herbicide. Use 10 percent (100 grain) vinegar (i.e., vinegar in which about 10 percent of the liquid is acidic acid) at full strength or soap herbicides as effective organic products on hot days. Be sure to clean vinegar thoroughly out of metal spray parts, as it is very corrosive.

Pruning. Remove dead, diseased, and conflicting limbs.

Don't overprune or make flush cuts, and don't paint cuts—
pruning paint slows the natural healing process and harbors
pathogens. If you must paint cuts, use natural shellac or, better
still, Lac Balsam.

Controlling aphids and other small pests. Build soil health
and release ladybugs, green lacewings, and trichogramma wasps.
Spray garlic tea as a preventative. Spray garlic/pepper tea if
needed. *Spider mites:* Spray liquid seaweed and fish emulsion
regularly and release green lacewings. Spray horticultural oil for
heavy infestations. *Caterpillars and bagworms: Bacillus thuringiensis* (Bt), Bt 'Israelensis' for mosquitoes. *Slugs, snails, fleas,
ticks, chinch bugs, roaches, crickets:* Diatomaceous earth/pyre-
thrum. *Whiteflies:* A mix of liquid seaweed and garlic/pepper tea.
Fire Ants: Logic or Award fire ant control for large areas, D.E./
pyrethrum on individual mounds. Soapy water is also effective.
Grubworms: beneficial nematodes are effective, but maintaining
healthy soil biology is the primary control. *Squash bugs, stink
bugs, and other hard-to-kill pests:* Sabadilla dust. *Roaches:* create bait stations using 50 percent Arm & Hammer detergent and
50 percent sugar. *Black spot, brown patch, powdery mildew:*
The best control is prevention through soil improvement and
avoidance of high-nitrogen fertilizers. Baking-soda and liquid-
copper sprays are effective. Natural apple cider vinegar at 1½
ounces (3 tablespoons) per gallon of water is also effective.

Making compost. A compost pile can be started at any time
of the year. Good ingredients include leaves, hay, grass clippings, tree trimmings, nongreasy food scraps, bark, sawdust,
rice hulls, weeds, nut hulls, and animal manure. Mix the ingredients together in a container of wood, hay bales, hog wire, or
concrete blocks, or simply pile the material on the ground. The
best mixture is 75–80 percent vegetative matter and 20–25 percent animal waste, although any mix will compost. The ingredients should be a mix of coarse- and fine-textured material. Avoid
having all the pieces of material the same size, since the variety
of sizes will help air to move through the pile. Oxygen is a critical ingredient. Turn the pile at least once a month; more often

speeds up the process. Keep the pile moist, roughly the moisture of a squeezed-out sponge. Compost is ready to use when the ingredients are no longer identifiable. The color will be dark brown, the texture soft and crumbly, and the aroma that of a forest floor. Use compost in all bed preparation and as a high-quality mulch around annuals and perennials.

USEFUL HOMEMADE RECIPES

Garlic/pepper tea insecticide. Liquefy 2 bulbs of garlic and 2 hot peppers in a blender ⅓ full of water. Strain the solids and add enough water to the garlic/pepper juice to make 1 gallon of concentrate. Use ¼ cup of concentrate per gallon of spray. For added strength, add 2 tablespoons of vegetable oil or horticultural oil to each gallon of water in the sprayer.

Garlic tea. Liquefy 2 bulbs of garlic in a blender. Strain out the solids and add enough water to the garlic juice to make 1 gallon of concentrate. Shake well before using, and add ¼ cup of the concentrate to each gallon of water in the sprayer.

Baking-soda fungicide. Mix 4 teaspoons (about 1 rounded tablespoon) of baking soda and 1 teaspoon of liquid soap or vegetable oil into 1 gallon of water. Spray lightly on foliage of plants afflicted with black spot, powdery mildew, brown patch, or other fungal diseases. Avoid overusing or pouring on the soil.

Vinegar fungicide. Mix 3 tablespoons of natural apple cider vinegar in 1 gallon of water.

Compost tea. Fill a 5-gallon or larger bucket with half compost and half water. Let sit 2–4 days, strain the solids out, and dilute to a light iced-tea color.

FLEA CONTROL—THE NATURAL WAY

If you are ready to stop dumping toxic chemicals on your lawn, gardens, carpets, furniture, pets, and yourself, here's my holistic (that means comprehensive) flea program:

Diet. Feed pets a balanced, nutritious diet of your own cooking or an organic pet food that does not contain chemical preservatives. Sprinkle a small amount of food-grade diatomaceous earth (1 percent or less) on the pet food daily. Add an additional small amount of brewer's yeast, bee pollen, garlic powder, or food-grade seaweed.

Cleaning. Vacuum frequently, rake and sweep dog runs and sleeping areas regularly, pick up and compost pet waste.

Outdoor treatment. Dust or spray D.E./pyrethrum on highly infested areas. Light dusting is better than heavy amounts. In liquid sprays, add 2 tablespoons D.E./pyrethrum to 1 gallon of water. Use only as needed to avoid killing beneficial insects. A better choice is to spray beneficial nematodes.

Exercise. If the pets don't get natural exercise from running and playing, walk them regularly. Healthy animals have a greater resistance to disease and insect pests.

Grooming. Bathe pets as needed, but only with mild, non-toxic soaps. Herbal shampoos are good. Leave shampoo on pets for 5 minutes before rinsing thoroughly. Brush pets regularly and use a flea comb to remove pests. Drown fleas in soapy water.

Indoor treatment. Treat infested carpets with D.E. or boric-acid products. For heavy infestations use citrus-oil products and growth regulators on carpets and furniture. Dirty, infested carpets should be cleaned or removed.

Pet treatment. Apply herbal powders of pennyroyal, eucalyptus, or rosemary. Treat heavy infestations with D.E./pyrethrum products; ready-to-use growth-regulator products such as Petcor and Ovitrol are also available for serious problems. Avoid using pennyroyal on cats.

Note: Remember, D.E. for pets and pests is not the same as swimming pool D.E. Buy food-grade D.E. only from your local organic retailer. Use all products, including organic ones, carefully. Overusing them is dangerous and lessens their effectiveness.

Myths of Organic Landscaping

There are many myths about organic farming, gardening, and landscaping. Let's put it another way. There's a ton of B.S. put out about organics; in fact, it's the only form of natural fertilizer spread by some folks . . .

Myth #1: Organic gardening is ugly and wild. Organic land-scape gardens in reality are lush, healthy, green, and gorgeous. I find that trees are particularly easy to grow organically, and since they are the most important living landscape element, their health translates into visual beauty. It's a terrible misconception that organic landscaping has a wild and messy look. Soft, natural gardens are certainly possible, but crisp, straight-lined, formal gardens are also easy to install and maintain organically. The most famous formal gardens in the world, the gardens of Versailles, were maintained organically until World War II, when most chemical plant-care products were introduced.

Myth #2. Organics cost more. Organic landscaping and gardening actually *saves* money. The cost savings result from fewer fertilizer applications, less spraying, less water use, and reduced loss of plant materials. Commercial growers will also have lower insurance costs and greatly reduced liability. Spraying is more effective because the organic sprays can help control insects and diseases and feed the soil and plants at the same time. Water savings result from the increased amounts of organic matter and microorganisms in the soil, and plant loss is reduced because stress from artificial products and lifeless soil is removed.

Myth #3. Organics are not safe. The organic method is, on the contrary, the safest approach. Botanical and biological pest controls, unless misused, do not harm people, pets, or the environment. Organic products include, but are not limited to, compost, manure-based fertilizers, natural rock powders, and pest-control products derived from natural materials such as garlic, neem, Bt, pyrethrum, and D.E. D.E. is dangerous to breathe in large quantities, but so are all dusty materials. Organic fertilizers include, but are not limited to, blood meal, bone meal, rock phosphate, fish emulsion, seaweed, earthworm castings, humic acid, lava sand, and animal manures. The best fertilizer of all is nature's own—compost. People who proclaim certain organic products to be more dangerous than artificial chemical compounds are simply proclaiming their own ignorance.

Myth #4: Organic products are not available. This used to be true, but now it's false. Wholesale outlets, retail stores, and mail-order catalogs are now selling large quantities of organic products. As recently as 1989, organic products were scarce in nurseries, hardware stores, and feed stores, but that's no longer the case. People have seen that The Natural Way works, and public pressure has forced the trades to respond.

Myth #5: Organics means natural. Not *completely* a myth, but not completely true either. Organic means using our understanding of nature as a guide for gardening and living, and growing food without the use of chemical pesticides or synthetic fertilizers. Organic techniques include any procedure or product that helps nature's balances stay in order and functioning properly.

Myth #6: Organics means more work. Organic landscaping actually requires less work once the soil has been brought back to a healthy condition—and besides, it's more fun. It does require learning something about soils, plant needs, and the life cycles of insects, but once it's in the blood, it becomes a great pastime and pleasure.

Myth #7. Pesticides shouldn't be a concern because there are dangerous natural toxins in food. This wins the prize as the champion dopey comment of the decade. Yes, there are natural toxins in foods—always have been, always will be—but why would that make it okay to add additional chemical poisons to our food, on top of the natural toxins already there?

Myth #8. Organics won't work on a large scale. To disprove this one, here are a few examples of successful, large-scale organic projects: Frito-Lay National Headquarters, Plano, Texas (300 acres), Johnson and Johnson Medical's office facility, Arlington, Texas (100 acres), Maddox Ranch, Colorado City, Texas (22,000 acres), Stahmann Farms, Las Cruces, New Mexico (3,000-acre pecan operation); Gallo Wines, throughout California (over 1,000 acres of vineyards); Fetzer Wines, Hopland, California (1,500 acres of vineyards). There are many other examples. The fact is, organic programs work *better* on a large scale because there is less negative impact from surrounding properties.

Myth #9. Organic products aren't university tested or legally registered. Many quality organic products have lots of university testing and have been registered for some time. Currently, new ones are being tested and registered every few weeks now. A great deal of both private and university testing is now under way around the world.

Myth #10. Organics is about killing pests with safer products. An organic lawn and/or tree program is not just a matter of doing away with chemical pesticides. It's an entirely different philosophy and attitude about how to select, plant, grow, and maintain plants. Traditional chemical programs are built around a "kill" philosophy. Synthetic pesticides are designed to provide an instant kill of bugs, weeds, and disease organisms. Organic programs, on the other hand, are built around a "health" philosophy which works over a longer period of time to solve the fundamental problems causing the attack of the pests. The fundamental problem is usually poor or unhealthy soil, inadequate drainage, or a combination of both. Poor plant selection can also be the culprit.

It's Not a Question of Chemicals versus Organics

I don't like to kill insects with organic pesticides much more than I like to kill them with chemical pesticides, but at least the organic alternatives are a more intelligent approach. It's best to avoid even the natural pesticides if possible because they, like the chemicals, kill beneficial as well as harmful insects. When allowed, insects will do a terrific job of controlling themselves. Only about 1 percent of the millions of different kinds of insects are really harmful. Even insects we think of as harmful are often providing an important function in the balance of nature.

The argument is not one of chemicals versus organics. Everything in the known universe is made up of, or is one of, the 92 basic elements on the chart that we were supposed to learn in high-school chemistry class. Air and water are made up primarily of the chemicals hydrogen, oxygen, nitrogen, and carbon.

The words "chemical" and "organic" are confusing. Some techniques and products acceptable for use in an organic program use synthetic chemicals, and some natural organic products are highly toxic and not acceptable in a wise organic program. But don't be confused. The point is that the two words have become the labels of the two opposing camps. The word "chemical" represents the traditional, university-approved approach of using artificial fertilizers and synthetic pesticides. The word "organic" represents the natural method of working with nature to improve soil health and maintain health and balance in all life.

Chemicals are not all bad. Some of the best tools in the organic gardener's arsenal are chemicals; the growth regulators for control of fire ants, roaches, and fleas are one example. They work by controlling the growth of insects, not by killing them, and they have very low toxicity to beneficial insects, pets, humans, and the environment; moreover, they biodegrade quickly.

On the other hand, some of the best natural tools of the organic gardener are extremely toxic materials, but they are targeted to specific pests. Bt (*Bacillus thuringiensis*) and Bti (*Bacillus thuringiensis* 'Israelensis') are highly toxic natural products that are used to kill caterpillars, beetles, mosquitoes, and other pests; they don't hurt beneficial insects, pets, humans, or the environment. Much research is currently under way to develop similar products to control roaches, potato beetles, whiteflies, aphids, and spider mites.

Another difference in philosophy relates to fertilization. The traditional attitude of proponents of chemical methods is that plants must be fertilized with a high-nitrogen fertilizer four times a year. The idea of balancing the soil is rarely, if ever, discussed. The organic philosophy, in contrast, is that the soil should be fed and balanced and that plants don't need to be force-fed.

Although D.E. or pyrethrum can be used as natural alternatives to Diazinon or Sevin to kill pests, the direct control of insects, diseases, and weeds is just a small part of an organic program. Organics is not about killing pests with safer insecticides; it is about reestablishing natural controls. An organic program avoids pest problems altogether by ensuring that preparation of the soil, planting, and maintenance of the soil and plants are all done properly. It's really all about common sense.

Traditional chemical programs are built around a philosophy of "kill the bugs." Organic programs are built around a philosophy that "soil health creates plant health," which works over a longer period of time to solve the fundamental problems that are causing the pest to attack. Such problems include unhealthy soil, inadequate drainage, too much or too little water or sunlight, or a combination of these. The only other fundamental problem in gardening, landscaping, or agriculture is poor plant choice. Successful horticulture and agriculture are greatly dependent upon the choice of well-adapted plant species.

Insect pests are only symptoms of the real problem. Homeowners and people in the landscape industry have developed a comforting belief that the synthetic sprays will quickly eliminate any visible insects, diseases, or weeds. Even though these products do not always totally eliminate the targeted pest, the suppliers can tell their clients that they have used the ultimate, most powerful weapons that technology has made available. With an organic program, the situation is different. The ultimate weapons have not been used. There is an unfortunate perception that the gentle organic techniques and products aren't the strongest or most effective solutions. Even though the reverse step of going back to chemicals is not beneficial either to plants or, more important, to the soil, it is an available choice.

In response to health and ecological issues, we are becoming less a quick-fix society and more inclined to favor what's best in the long run. The impact of quick fixes on the environment and on the health of people is now a mainstream concern. Even the politicians are jumping on the bandwagon because the public pressure is mounting daily.

Several decades ago, Sir Albert Howard said that there is only one real cause of disease—malnutrition. I believe that theory in general, and it is definitely the case in landscaping and gardening. Soil that is healthy by virtue of a balance of organic matter, rock minerals, and living organisms will transfer its energy up into the plants, and those plants will have a natural resistance to insects and disease. Healthy landscape plants are easy to maintain, and healthy food crops pass their nutrition and energy on to animals and ultimately to people. That healthy balance of nutrition works very effectively to prevent disease.

Even though there has been a controversy over terminology, I decided to use "organic" to describe this alternative philosophy because it can be more clearly understood than "Earth kind," "biodynamic," "eco-agriculture," "integrated pest management" (IPM), "low input sustainable agriculture" (LISA), or any of the other ecological and less toxic meaning terms. The words "health," "balance," and "ecological" would be more accurate terms, but I will continue to use "organic" because it seems to have the clearest connotation and the best chance of promoting the idea of using alternative techniques and products that are less toxic, more effective, and more inclined to help maintain nature's balances.

Me and Organics

My wife, Judy, wants me to stop reading and researching so much. It seems to her that the more I learn, the more I discover what's wrong and the more concerned I get about the world. It appears to her that every new bit of information points out another depressing problem—water pollution, air pollution, unhealthy food, diminishing resources, pesticide buildup, loss of biodiversity, and on and on. She's afraid it could become overwhelming, but the more I learn, the clearer the picture becomes. I now see that great progress is being made—not always for the right reasons, but it is progress nonetheless. Irresponsible people continue to deny that environmental problems exist, but their voices become dimmer by the day.

I try to avoid crying out about the negative aspects of the last fifty years of horticulture and agriculture, based, as they have been, on the use of toxic chemicals. Instead, I try to spend my time addressing the positives of organics and teaching others how to use techniques that work better. I started my serious education in organics in 1985. Yes, I used to be an environmental thug before I became an environmental wacko. It was hard to spread the word at first because there was no university backup, just the advice of wise people—gardeners, landscapers, ranchers, and farmers. The answers were simple and easy, maybe too easy. Organic methods work because nature works. Nature is perfect. Brave people trying my seemingly wild ideas found that they worked for them, they passed the information on to their friends, and the word spread quickly. I had invented nothing. These organic techniques were as old as life itself. History shows that the Celts in Ireland were using them as early as 3000 years B.C. Many once-prosperous civilizations have failed because they abandoned the natural approach to agriculture. I'm not going to get into what's wrong with agriculture in the United States, but the simple fact is that we had better learn from history or we too will fail.

I broke out of the crowd years ago. It never made sense to me to plant the same five plants on each project or to use some of the planting and maintenance techniques everyone else seemed to think were right. Instead, I questioned their use and began to adopt new approaches.

I became organic the day I first saw my nine-month-old daughter, Logan, pick up everything she saw and stick it in her mouth. I didn't know how to "do" organics, but I was going to find out. I called my friend Alex Burton—I figured he knew something about organics—his front yard certainly looked organic. He suggested that I call the Texas Department of Agriculture. I met Beth Bettinger. She suggested the beginning of the rest of the story.

Beth, who was a cheerleader for the organic movement, had me call John Dromgoole, one of the country's best-known organic practitioners. He, in turn, introduced me to Malcolm Beck, who not only became a friend but introduced me to the organic way of life. Malcolm is a longtime organic gardener and farmer from San Antonio. He is one of the most knowledgeable in the country on compost and taught me how to make it. He also taught me that every living thing sooner or later dies and everything that dies, rots. On the surface, that sounds pretty morbid. In reality, though, it is fundamental to understanding life, nature, and organics. If dead things didn't rot, this earth would be several thousand feet deep in dead bodies and a smelly place indeed. Malcolm taught me that the decaying process returns plants and animals back to the earth and into the raw elements from which they were made. On their journey back, these basic minerals become the nutrition and vitality to feed the next generation of plants and animals. The decaying process, better called the disassembling process, is performed by the billions of tiny creatures in the soil we call microorganisms or microbes. With or without our help, these microorganisms can turn our once-living organic debris into fertilizer for our farms and gardens. They can, that is, if they are allowed to do so. Unfortunately, however, in most cities vegetative waste in the form of tree trimmings, leaves, grass clippings, and the like is usually buried in landfills where these life-sustaining nutrients are locked away from air, as well as the natural life, death, and decay cycle. Such waste, which could have greatly benefitted the fertility and well-being of the soil, has become a great environmental problem from two standpoints: We are mining these resources and depleting them from the soil, and we are continuing to create giant anaerobic garbage dumps out of them.

I still hear the tired old statement that plants don't care whether the fertilizer nutrients are from organic or chemical sources. Well, not only do the plants care, but so do the microbes, the insects, the soil, the animals, and the people. To say that plants don't care about the source of nutrients is as ridiculous as saying that people don't care if their nutrients come from pills and shots rather than from whole foods. Nature is not a composite of a bunch of independent pieces. Nature is a whole, a complete system in which everything is related to everything else. Hurting any small part of nature hurts everything and everyone.

In Malcolm Beck's book *The Garden-Ville Method*, it's clear right from the start that he is a well-educated fellow, not from formal schooling, but from personal experience, trial and error, and experimentation. Malcolm has taken the time to watch and understand nature. He has learned the secrets of soil management by reading the books of soil experts such as Sir Albert Howard and Dr. William A. Albrecht and by working the soil with his own hands during his thirty years as an organic truck farmer and compost maker. It has not been an easy road. Some called him crazy, while others just ignored him, but he never gave up. He never gave up because he knew he was right. He understood nature's laws and learned to work within those laws.

Although powerful organizations have been and still are a big challenge to independent-thinking people like Malcolm Beck, battles are being won, and the overall victory is in sight. Mainstream, chemical-rescue farming and horticulture are coming unglued because they don't work, especially over the long haul, and at the same time, organic, ecological agriculture and horticulture are taking over. Why? Because working within nature's systems works better, and because people like Malcolm Beck have proved that it does.

Malcolm is a very special naturalist and teacher in that he is completely open with his knowledge and skills and will help anyone. His philosophy is that God doesn't help those who keep secrets, and that knowledge is the property of nature, not of people, and certainly not of any one person. Malcolm also accepts the fact that we will make mistakes, and that we must continue to learn, adjust, and adapt. I know of his willingness to share and to teach and to continue to learn because, you see, I am his pupil.

Rachel Carson Was Right

Although I never had the pleasure of meeting her, Rachel Carson, the author of *Silent Spring*, had a strong influence on my conversion to organics. She set the wheels of common sense in motion. Many people have been introduced to the dangers of our current agricultural and horticultural practices by reading her book. Written in 1962, *Silent Spring* warned us in a very clear way about what had already happened to the fragile balance of our environment and what the future held if we didn't change our ways.

Rachel Carson's message was simple. She warned us, not about single, heavy doses of pesticides, but rather about small, repeated exposures that ultimately destroy the balances in nature and cause serious diseases and other health problems for wild animals, pets, and people. To this day we are still seeing the damage wrought by DDT on specific animal species and the environment in general.

On December 4, 1962, with the reaction to the publication of *Silent Spring* at its height, Rachel Carson spoke to the National Women's Press Club on the nature of the response and her experience with the wide publicity. Her most interesting comment during that speech was that "no one in several county farm offices who was talked to today had read the book, but all disapproved of it heartily." Although she said it in her lighthearted way, she was deadly serious.

Carson described the attack on her book as falling into a rather definite pattern and as employing all the well-known devices. "One obvious way to weaken a cause is to discredit the person who champions it. And so, the masters of invective have been busy. I am a bird lover, a cat lover, a fish lover, I am a priestess of nature, and I am a devotee of some mystical cult that has to do with laws of the universe which my critics somehow consider themselves immune to. Another well-known and much-used device is to misrepresent my position and then to attack the things that I have never said. Now, I don't want to belabor the obvious, because anyone who has really read the book knows that I do favor insect control in appropriate situations; that I do not advocate the complete abandonment of chemical control; that I criticize modern chemical control, not because it controls harmful insects, but because it controls them badly and inefficiently and because it creates many dangerous side effects in doing so. I criticize the present methods because they are based on a rather low-level of scientific thinking—we really are capable of much greater sophistication in our solution of this problem." These words should be ordered to be on the office walls of anyone specifying pest-control chemicals.

Carson also noted the existence of other reminders that unsafe chemicals get into use and gave the example of county agents who frequently had to amend or rescind earlier advice on the use of pesticides. (Such retractions continue today, with many previously approved pesticides being removed from the recommendation lists. Cities are finding unacceptable levels of diazinon in the waste water, and chemical lawn care companies are eliminating 2,4-D, fungicides, and soil sterilants from their arsenals.) Carson went on:

"It's also worthy of notice that during the years of 1959, 1960, and 1961, airplane crashes involving crop-dusting planes totaled 873. In these accidents, 135 pilots lost their lives. This fact led to some very significant research by the Federal Aviation Agency through its Civil Aeronautic Aeromedical Unit. The report contained two very significant facts: (1) there is a causal relation between the buildup of toxins in the cell and the onset of sugar diabetes; (2) the build-up of poisons within the cell interferes with the rate of energy production in the human body." Crop-duster planes are still flying, and they are still spewing chemical poisons all over the country, but there is closer inspection of the number and type of chemicals.

Rachel Carson was largely responsible for getting DDT taken off the market, at least in this country. We owe her a lot but have much work left to do to get the rest of the unnecessary toxic poisons off the market.

Organics and Budgets

There are those who say that organic programs cost too much. Those people are wrong. Organic techniques actually save money. It's a common misconception, unfortunately, that organic products and techniques cost more money and require more labor to apply than chemicals. If you compare a bag of chemical fertilizer with a bag of organic fertilizer, the organic stuff does usually cost more. But wait a minute—there are other considerations. First of all, you don't have to put the organic stuff out as often, and, second, organic programs provide additional, indirect savings related to such factors as lower water use, greater plant and flower production, and less plant loss—all a result of healthier soil. In the long run, in fact, an organic program offers considerable savings.

Some of the costs are saved by fertilizing less often, spraying for pests less often, spending less on planting, replacing fewer sick and dead plants, and watering less. Cost savings result, too, from knowing what steps to take first. Although organic programs cost less in the long run, there can be a temporary increase in maintenance costs during the transition from a chemical program. While it's ideal to spend some extra money up front to increase the soil health quickly, it's not essential, and options exist that can make a project as economical as it needs to be. A phased approach, for example, is more commonly used and is often more practical. When using such an approach, always start a program by implementing phases that have the most impact. The first step is to correct or eliminate the most limiting factors, of which there can be many, though in unhealthy soils the most common one is usually the lack of oxygen in the top 7 inches. The exchange of gases, with oxygen moving down into the soil and carbon dioxide moving up and out of the soil, is critical for the rest of the natural systems in the soil to function properly.

The soil must be well aerated for the roots of plants and the microorganisms to thrive, and the microorganisms must be healthy in order for the soil to have the proper water-holding capacity and for sufficient nutrients to be released. Aeration can be done mechanically by hole punching, tilling, or subsurface ripping.

The next most common factor limiting soil health in gardens, lawns, parks, and golf courses is the overuse of artificial, salt-based fertilizers. Switching to organic fertilizers is the solution. Organic fertilizers are better for the soil because not only do they provide immediately available and slow-release nutrients, but they also benefit the soil by adding organic matter which becomes humus and a wide range of trace minerals. Implementing these steps helps the beneficial living organisms in the soil. If the microbes are thriving, the air will penetrate deeper into the soil, drainage will improve, the proper amount of moisture will be held longer, and the tied-up nutrients will be released more readily.

Soil temperature is also a common limiting factor and is best controlled through mulching. Mulching buffers the soil temperature from highs and lows. A layer of organic litter on the soil also helps to maintain soil moisture, eliminate weed problems, and prevent erosion and compaction from heavy rains. Thick mulches that are at least 4–6 inches deep are best, but it's wise to avoid piling the mulch up against the trunks of shrubs and trees, since the constant moisture against it can rot the bark.

Organiphobia

Why are the majority of homeowners and landscape professionals still using the chemical approach even though the organic approach has proven so successful on residential and commercial properties? It's a good question—it's the one I'm asked most often—and it has a complicated answer. Organic techniques aren't yet used by all homeowners because much of the industry still pushes chemicals instead of organics. The reason for that is that many industry people are afraid of organics. They are organiphobes. Some are afraid even of the *term* "organics." Organiphobes have a fear of organics for five basic reasons.

1. Organic techniques aren't understood. Organiphobes know how to recommend and use the chemical products, but they can't answer the questions about organic products. Organic products and techniques are not usually covered in university research or featured in the traditional industry publications, and some products don't have labels that explain their use. In addition, no comprehensive organic program is being taught at any major university.

2. *Profit from chemical sales.* Many people make money from the sale of chemicals. Those whose income results directly or indirectly from the sale of artificial pesticides and fertilizers are usually organiphobes. You can't blame them—they have to pay the bills, after all, and at stake here are advertising money, commissions, research grant money, cash flow, and basic salaries.

3. *Paradigm problems.* Many people can't see what we're talking about. They are not stupid; they just can't see it at all. Organic thoughts are simply not in their world—not within their set of rules, or paradigms. Paradigms are boundaries that are set for us by our parents, their parents, customs, and history. Here's a good example. For about 100 years prior to 1968 the Swiss controlled 65 percent of the world watch industry and 80 percent of its profits. Swiss-made watches were the standard in the industry. In 1968 the Swiss watchmakers' own scientists recommended a revolutionary change in watches—electric watches. The Swiss owners laughed, saying, "This is not a watch—it has no mainspring, no gears—how silly!" They thought the idea was so bad, they didn't even protect it. Japanese watchmakers, seeing the electric watches at a conference, thought the idea was pretty good—and the rest is history. The Japanese now dominate the industry, and the Swiss control less than 10 percent of the market.

To organiphobes, organic techniques are just not worth considering as proper horticulture and agriculture. Such people can't see how significantly the world is changing, nor can they see that working with nature is much easier and more cost effective than trying to dominate it.

4. *Fear of loneliness.* Most people feel intimidated about going against the grain, being mavericks or pioneers. It's comforting to be doing what others are doing—even if it's wrong. With the organic approach, each person needs to accept more responsibility and be comfortable working within natural laws and systems. Some organic tools—such as compost, air, and mulch—don't have detailed labels or EPA registration. If something goes wrong or doesn't work with a chemical product, the blame can be laid off or the monkey can be handed to someone else; the landscaper can say that the nursery recommended it, the nursery can say that the extension service recommended it, and the extension service can say that it worked on their isolated tests or that it worked on the manufacturer's test. Whether the product worked or not is beside the point. You can say the best industry recommendations have been used, so it's not your fault if it doesn't work. With organics you have to take the responsibility yourself. Since the majority of people in landscaping, horticulture, and agriculture have no formal training or research in organics, they are uncomfortable with that much responsibility.

5. ***Inability to admit being wrong.*** This may be the most powerful obstacle. It's difficult for anyone to admit to a mistake. The bigger the mistake, the harder the admission. The biggest critics of organics are those who are the most schooled in using the "treat-the-symptom-with-artificial-products" approach. Some PhDs understand nature's workings, but many focus only on their specialty and don't consider nature as a whole. My teacher, Malcolm Beck, didn't go to college at all. He worked for the railroad and became an organic farmer on the side. He simply watched nature, read, and learned; yet he can now explain the overall organic way of living and the details of organics probably better than anyone.

I have not been organic all my life. I started learning about organics in 1985, and until 1988 I used some synthetic pesticides and artificial fertilizers. When I was exposed to the complete alternative approach, I was hooked immediately—it just made so much sense. I'd been wrong for many years, from the time I started my career in golf-course maintenance in 1970 until my complete conversion. I was lucky; some people have been using and preaching "better life through chemistry" for much longer—some for as long as fifty years (no longer than fifty years because, for the most part, artificial chemicals for use in agricultural and landscape products were born out of World War II). It's hard to admit you've been imparting bad advice for the bulk of your life.

Today dozens of large-scale commercial projects use totally organic programs, many landscape contractors practice organics, hundreds of small commercial projects are under way, and thousands of organic residential gardens are thriving. Yet organiphobia persists, and unfortunately, the organiphobes still have majority control—but maybe not for much longer. Every day I meet more people who are listening, asking questions, and trying organic techniques. Toxic-chemical rescue is on the decline, and organic methods are gathering momentum. The reason is simple: The Natural Way works best.

2 Soil Management

The Living Soil

No matter what term is used—natural, ecological, organic, least toxic, integrated pest management (IPM), sustainable, low input—the point of this alternative philosophy is just plain common sense and good horticulture. As I mentioned earlier, I prefer the term "organic" because it seems to be the most easily understood. Organics is about the soil, about plants, and, most important, about natural systems that have existed since the beginning of time.

There are many reasons why organic methods aren't more universally understood and used. For one thing, nature and science have for some time been out of sync. The sciences of botany and zoology teach only about the growing half of life and don't touch on the other half—death and decay. Therein lies our failure to understand and use nature's powerful and resilient systems, which work on a continuing cycle of birth to death to birth again. While some might call it recycling, its correct name is *life*.

Organics and the elimination of waste have now become popular on a global scale and the 1990s will definitely be remembered as the decade of the environmentalist. The increasing pressure from radio, television, newspapers, and magazines, the EPA's tightening of the reins, and, most important, the power of concerned farmers, ranchers, and homeowners have all made finding safer, more environmentally sensitive solutions to raising crops of all kinds a mainstream political and economic concern.

Solving landfill problems and reducing the amounts of dangerous chemicals used in farming, landscaping, and grounds maintenance are all well and good, but they're not the main reasons I'm so excited. The most fascinating aspect of organics is this—it works *better* than the toxic chemical and artificial alternatives! The fact that organic techniques and products help us stop ruining our planet is a welcome side benefit.

Understanding in detail how nature's systems work is difficult because those systems are complex. However, it's easy to put conditions in place that allow nature's systems to work effectively on their own, and to convert property of any size from an artificial program to an organic program. It can be done on golf courses, parks, college campuses, and commercial developments as well as on home farms and landscapes. Here's how it works.

Healthy soil produces healthy plants. Healthy plants in turn produce pleasure and health in animals and people. It's a simple formula, but it works. Traditional chemical landscape programs treat plants directly and artificially, similar to the way sick people are kept alive by drugs and machines. Soil-health programs feed plants indirectly through a natural and balanced process similar to the way people are nourished on healthy, balanced diets.

Soil is the key to health. There's a big difference between a healthy, living soil and inert, lifeless dirt. Healthy soil is a dynamic, constantly changing complex system of air, water, minerals, organic matter, and living organisms. It is a fascinating balance of growth and decay with a complex metabolism that can be easily damaged or destroyed by the misuse of artificial products. Soil's volume is generally made up of about 50 percent air and water (combined), while slightly less than 50 percent consists of decomposed rock minerals. Organic matter contributes 3–6 percent of the soil's volume, while its live constituents (small plants, animals, and other microorganisms) account for less than 1 percent. It is the balance of all these soil ingredients that determines plants' natural pest and disease resistance. The magic of soil health works equally well for agricultural crops, ornamental plantings, and potted plants. It's so simple, it's hard to believe.

Much of the land in the United States and other countries has been overworked, poisoned, overfertilized, sterilized, mined, compacted, and eroded. All that devastation through the years changes soil to dirt. A simple definition of dirt is "dead soil." Trees, shrubs, groundcovers, vines, perennials, and annuals, together with vegetables and other agricultural crops, have been kept alive and growing by life-support techniques and chemical products—insecticides, fungicides, herbicides, and harsh chemical fertilizers.

An incredible misconception exists that chemicals are good for plants. In truth, synthetic products are medicines to treat symptoms, not cures for major ailments, the most common of which is unhealthy or dead soil. Two thousand years ago, societies were working with the soil carefully and allowing its powers to produce crops plentifully through the natural process. Some cultures still do that today, but in this country we have listened to the chemical companies and extension agents, and as a result we have polluted and overworked and taken from the soil without giving anything back for so long that we have reduced the soil to a near-sterile medium.

To understand how to create and maintain healthy soil, the basic components must be understood.

Soil structure. Solid materials make up about 50 percent of soil volume; the rest consists of pores filled with air and water. In clay or silt soils both the particles and the pores are small, whereas in sandy soils both particles and pores are large, though the total quantity of pore space is less than it is in soils with fine particles.

Soil compaction is a common problem related to soil structure. It results from chemical overuse, poor irrigation practices, mechanical or foot traffic, and other poor cultural practices and prevents the proper transfer of soil gases and the normal growth of roots. Compacted soil puts at least 50 percent of the fertility cycle out of action. Without oxygen in the soil, humus formation cannot proceed. The organic program alone will correct compaction in time, but to speed the process, and to heal damaged turf and expand biodiversity, mechanical aeration is recommended.

Air and water. The importance of these constituents of healthy soil cannot be overemphasized, so it is indeed unfortunate that the liquid and gaseous parts of the soil are often ignored. Air and water have to be able to move freely through the soil for the natural systems to function. While mechanical solutions such as aeration are sometimes needed in the beginning for compacted soil, land with a natural balance of ingredients will have good aggregation, positive drainage, and water-retention ability, all provided by the living portion of the soil.

Organic matter. Organic matter comes from many sources, including plant and animal wastes and the dead bodies of small animals, insects, and microorganisms. There is normally four times more plant or vegetable waste on the forest floor than there is animal waste. Sources of organic matter for the compost pile or for bed preparation or for the forest floor include leaves, sawdust, bark, roots of plants, root exudates, weeds, algae, cover crops, animal urine and manure, agricultural waste, nut hulls, dead animals, trash, and water plants. Organic matter is decomposed primarily through the feeding of microorganisms, and it is this natural process that creates humus, the secret key to healthy soil.

Humus is a dark-brown-to-black substance that is nearly insoluble and nonfibrous, and that contains about 30 percent each of lignin, protein, and complex sugars. It is shapeless, does not resemble the parent material, contains 3–5 percent nitrogen (N) and 55–60 percent carbon (C), and has a carbon-to-nitrogen (C:N) ratio of 10:1.

Humus is never static but is constantly being transformed by natural processes into humic acid, vitamins, enzymes, and minerals. It is the source of food and energy supporting the development of microorganisms and is the stage of decomposition that provides food for plants in the form of slow-release nitrogen, phosphorus, sulfur, and all other elements. Humus is like Jell-O in soil. Jell-O is made of sugar and water, yet the sugar doesn't drain away and the water doesn't leak out—you can hold Jell-O without getting your hand wet. Humus holds the soil nutrients in the same way, keeping them from volatilizing into air or leaching away.

To bring dead or dying soil back to life, start by adding compost to all your planting beds and lawn areas. The best organic material is compost because it contains so many microorganisms, enzymes, and nutrients for immediate use in the soil. The amount isn't critical—you can spread anywhere from ½ inch to 12 inches—although more *is* better in this case. Use as much as you can afford to buy, or even better, use your own homemade compost. The magic will start to happen almost immediately. The improved health of your plants will begin to show right away because compost provides humus, humic acid, and enzymes that not only encourage growth but also kill harmful pathogens and diseases. You'll be amazed at the dramatic change you will see and feel—you'll be able to tell that the plants like what you are up to. You will also notice that the addition of compost in your planting beds and even in grass areas will help to hold the moisture in the soil at a much more even level, and your water bills will go down.

Minerals. Minerals come primarily from weathered rock. The mineral portion of the soil includes stones, decayed rocks, sand, silt, and clay, which are the natural sources of potash, phosphorus, and many other naturally occurring elements. Minerals provide food for microorganisms and a slow-release supply of nutrients; they are supplied to the topsoil from the base rock of the area, whether it's limestone, granite, or sandstone. Rock minerals of volcanic origin are added to unbalanced soils to increase their water-holding capacity and nutrient-exchange capacity and their trace-mineral availability. Volcanic-rock minerals such as lava sand will also increase the energy of the soil by collecting and redistributing cosmic energy, which is primarily the energy from the sun.

Microorganisms. Even though healthy soil contains only a small percentage of microorganisms, they are critical, and maybe the most important constituent to understand. These tiny plants and animals are born, live, feed, and die in the soil. Soil-born microscopic flora and fauna include bacteria, fungi, actinomycetes, algae, protozoa, yeast, nematodes, germs, and many other tiny critters. Yes, there are good and bad microorganisms, but if you don't foul up the natural systems with toxic materials, the beneficial microbes will prevail over the harmful and destructive ones.

A healthy soil has a constantly changing but always active and balanced population of microbes. There are approximately 900,000,000,000 (nine hundred billion) of these life-forms in every one pound of soil. Bacteria are rich in protein and help to produce nitrogen and nitrates; they also encourage biochemical reactions in soil and have a strong influence on plant growth. Mycorrhizal fungi contain as much as 10 percent nitrogen and take on various forms—they are sometimes nodules, and sometimes white, cobweblike threads that actually attach to roots and enter the cells of root hairs, where they are then absorbed into the plant. They extend, enlarge (by as much as one million times), and make more efficient the root systems of plants. They do not exist in healthy populations in sterile planting mixtures or in dead soil.

In general, unbalanced sandy soils drain too fast, while unbalanced clay soils hold too much water; their lack of balance is often due to an absence of organic matter and living organisms. Microorganisms are a vital part of physical soil balance, and they are encouraged by the use of organic products and the avoidance of chemical poisons and artificial fertilizers. Microorganisms feed on organic matter and form gluelike nutrient sugars, called polysaccharides, which weld individual soil particles together, creating larger particles or aggregates. It is this process that gives soil its wonderful feel, or tilth, and its pleasant forest-floor fragrance.

Our Friends the Earthworms

Besides the billions of microscopic plants and animals in each cubic foot of healthy soil, there are lots of macroorganisms—the organisms we can see, such as spiders, centipedes, millipedes, springtails, and other insects and critters. The most fascinating and helpful of these is the earthworm. Earthworms—or night crawlers as some people call them—inhabit the cool, moist soil in the garden and have a much more important role than as fishing bait. They are good friends because they provide nutrients and improve the structure of the soil for other beneficial soil life.

Earthworms—long neglected, or even killed as a nuisance—have been "rediscovered" as the world's best soil builders. These "intestines of the soil," as Aristotle called them, break up soil hardpans, drill miles of burrows which soak up fast-falling rains, help plants root more deeply into the soil, shift chemically unbalanced soils toward a neutral pH, create fertilizer nutrients, and loosen compaction.

A single earthworm deposits its weight in castings every twenty-four hours. That may not seem like a lot, but earthworms in an acre of soil are able to produce about 15 tons of castings in one year. That amount is roughly equivalent to three hundred dollars' worth of a well-balanced chemical fertilizer with the N-P-K analysis of roughly 10-20-10 plus trace elements. The nitrogen, calcium, magnesium, phosphorus, and potassium levels are considerably higher in earthworm castings than in surrounding soil without castings. The earthworms also help increase soil microorganisms, while they destroy the harmful fungi, bacteria, and root nematodes as they digest them.

The earthworm's digestive system also helps to neutralize soil that is either too acidic or too alkaline. Even Charles Darwin discovered and commented on the great importance of earthworms, stating that vegetation in many parts of the world would be eliminated without their helpful benefits.

Earthworms are attracted to soils that are high in organic matter and free from pesticides and harsh chemical fertilizers. Earthworms can be purchased from growers or grown at home in moist compost. In order to help keep them in a confined area while you are "raising" them, feed them periodically with cornmeal. This will prevent them from leaving the compost "nursery" until you are ready to introduce them to your garden or landscaped area. Growing your own earthworms or adding them to your garden can be enjoyable, but they will return naturally and increase in number rapidly if you stop using chemicals and go organic!

Our earthworm friends enrich soil and improve its productivity in many ways and at the same time help balance the natural systems in the earth. The following are some of the areas in which the earthworm makes specific contributions.

Water absorption. Earthworms improve the aggregation and tilth of the soil, so that even hard rains soak in instead of running off and eroding the ground. They dig pencil-sized vertical tunnels, allowing rainfall to flow deeply into the subsoil. Water runs through the worm tunnels and seeps slowly from these underground conduits into surrounding soil, and as a result the entire root zone is more evenly moistened. These same tunnels also help to prevent waterlogged, anaerobic conditions, which is very important in heavy clay soils.

Aeration. From the surface to a depth of 3–5 feet, by way of their tunnels, earthworms bring oxygen down to stimulate microbial conversion of minerals into plant nutrients. The aerobic depth of the soil is increased, and carbon dioxide is more effectively moved up to the soil surface and released. The linings of worms' tunnels are rich with polysaccharides which, with their gluelike consistency, help the tunnels remain in place for several years. Air, nutrients, and the rich bacterial life associated with the tunnels encourage root growth.

Root-growth stimulation. The creation by earthworms of a horizontal network of tunnels enables roots to grow 6–7 inches a day through otherwise compacted soil. As root residue fills these tunnels, deep moisture moves up through them by osmosis to feed roots nearer the surface; the root system becomes more extensive as a result of easy growth through these "pipelines."

Tilling. Earthworms pull scraps of raw and decaying organic matter down from the ground surface into the network of underground passages. This process mixes the debris thoroughly with the soil and helps to digest the raw residue and convert it to nutrient-rich humus and other compounds needed by plants.

Hormones. Earthworms break down crop-growth inhibitors such as phenols and formaldehyde from decaying residue and lace the processed material with plant-growth stimulants containing growth regulators or hormones such as auxins and cytokinins. Earthworms can treat 50 tons of soil per acre each year, or about 5 percent of the total weight of the top 6 inches of soil. In twenty years, they can completely process the entire topsoil layer. Earthworms place deposits of nutrient-laden castings throughout the soil, encouraging vigorous root growth.

Minerals. Earthworms help convert minerals into water-soluble, plant-available forms. This action makes calcium, nitrogen, phosphorus, potassium, and other elements more available to plants. Processed deposits left by earthworms contain five to ten times as many soluble plant nutrients as the original soil. Under good working conditions, worms can process and bring to the surface a half-inch of finely textured, stone-free, mineral-rich soil each year.

Soil pH. Soil processed by earthworms is always more balanced and usually closer to neutral pH than the original soil, whether acid or alkaline.

Microorganisms. Earthworm bodies contain compartments which multiply microorganisms, distribute them along the passageways, and spread them on the surface to help decompose organic matter.

Tilth. Healthy soil contains sugars and enzymes which weld soil particles into clumps or aggregates. The physical change in the soil improves its water-holding capacity, aeration, and fertility.

Insects & pathogens. Earthworms create soil conditions that discourage populations of harmful nematodes and other plant pathogens. As earthworms help to improve the balance of the soil, the beneficial insects and microorganisms flourish.

Micronutrients. Worms help to chelate such minerals as

zinc, iron, and boron, linking these essential elements chemically with other plant nutrients so roots can easily absorb them. In other words, earthworms help to free tied-up nutrients and make them available to plants.

Thatch. Earthworms help to eliminate thatch problems by eating and digesting plant debris and by helping microorganisms convert small pieces of organic matter into humus.

To have more earthworms, feed them organic fertilizers and manures, avoid excessive tillage, mulch all bare soil, and avoid chemical fertilizers and pesticides; earthworms will repopulate naturally if they aren't poisoned. They are especially active during mild weather when the soil is moist. They stay deep in the soil during the heat of summer and the cold of winter. Treat them kindly and they will reward you.

THE EARTHWORM SOIL TEST

I have a new soil test, the earthworm test, to recommend, since what we organic gardeners should be most concerned about is the level of life in the soil. Dig out of the ground a section of soil measuring 12 inches along the sides and 6 inches deep and slowly sift it into a box, bucket, or wheelbarrow. Count the earthworms you see in the ½ cubic foot of soil. If your test is in turf, there should be at least six; if it is in a mulched bed area, there should be about ten. They should be big earthworms—about the size of your little finger. If your test doesn't uncover enough worms, or if they are puny, your soil is not healthy enough.

The presence of lots of big, plump earthworms shows that nature has been working and has filled the soil with life. If you see lots of worms, you can rest assured that the beneficial microbes are there, too. If the soil is full of life, the chemistry can't be too far from balanced and the same goes for the physical properties of the soil—if the earthworms are present, it will be well aerated and aggregated. Earthworm-rich soil will drain better but hold just the right amount of water significantly longer. Wait until you see the resulting improvement in plant growth.

Building a Healthy Soil

Re-creating healthy soil is done by establishing conditions in which nature can do what nature was designed to do. Most unhealthy soils have two major deficiencies: a lack of air and a lack of humus (broken-down organic matter). As a result, they usually have a low or imbalanced population of microorganisms, as well as an imbalance of chemical nutrients. Improving any one of these deficiencies immediately improves the others.

Step one in balancing soil is to get some air in the ground. Large acreage can be ripped or chisel plowed. Commercial and residential turf areas can be mechanically aerated with machines that punch holes. Hand-cultivating tools can be used to aerate ornamental beds with existing plants, while aeration of new beds or gardens can be achieved with a rototiller or cultivator.

The next step is to have the soil tested for chemical makeup. While soil samples may be collected any time, the best time is late winter, prior to the first fertilizer application. *If no samples have been taken within the last two years, however, the best time to test is right away.* Soil testing should be done annually and at the same time each year. The soil test will show what fertilizer nutrients are lacking and should be added to your program.

SOIL TESTING

Maps. Prepare an accurate drawing showing the location of the samples; this allows your sampling to be repeated from year to year. Give each of the areas sampled a name, letter, or number. Each test area should have about the same plant type (i.e., beds, turf, etc.). Any area that is different in slope, texture, color, drainage, or erosion history and that is large enough to be fertilized separately should be sampled and tested separately.

Collection. Use a soil probe, trowel, or sharpshooter to remove a sliver of soil 6–7 inches long (4 inches for no-till farms, pastures, and lawns). Shake the soil loose from any grass or thatch and put into a soil sample bag or clean, sealable plastic container. Never reuse sample bags, and never use any container that could have possible contamination, such as grocery sacks, bread wrappers, or old buckets. Take a minimum of five soil probes per composite sample for small areas, and one probe for every one or two acres from larger areas. Collect about ½ pound of soil for each sample. Samples may be sent in dry or wet.

Labeling. Put the name or identifying letter or number on each sample bag. Make sure the labeling on the bag matches the number of the representative area on the map. Label the bags to match the areas before taking the samples.

Testing Lab. Send the samples to a soil-testing service that gives not only detailed information about the chemical makeup of the soil, but also organic fertilizer recommendations. Two such companies are Texas Plant and Soil Labs, Route 7, Box 213 Y, Edinburg, TX 78539, and Timberleaf, 5569 State Street, Albany, OH 45710.

Best Beds

During my twenty years of designing, installing, and consulting on landscape projects, I have tried every conceivable formula, including chemical ones, for bed preparation. I've used peat moss, pine bark, sand, sandy loam, calcined clay, rice hulls, and lots of other stuff. The specifications and instructions in my earlier books vary from what I'm now recommending, for the simple reason that I have continued to learn better methods—not to mention the fact that, in the beginning, I didn't know what I was doing—I simply specified what everyone else was specifying.

Folks in the landscape business have a habit of staying with the same products and procedures if they seem to be working; after all, it's sometimes hard to admit that maybe there's a better way and that maybe a new approach would produce better results. While at one time I was no exception, it's not the approach I adopt now. Thus, from all my experiments and landscape projects, the following is what currently seems to me to be the best and what I recommend—at least until a better idea pops up.

ORGANIC BED PREPARATION

Step 1. Remove weeds & grass. Scrape away all weeds and grass, including rhizomes (the underground stems). About 2–3 inches deep is usually enough. A sod cutter can be used for this. *Do not use herbicides to kill the existing grass and weeds*; since undesirable plants must be dug out whether they are green or brown, save the money and avoid the chemicals.

Step 2. Establish the proper grade. If the grade needs to be adjusted, add native topsoil to all beds to about 2 inches below the adjacent finished grade. Don't add sharp sand, loam, or any other foreign, unnatural materials or soils that are different in color and texture from the native soil. With the exception of raised beds, new beds rarely need additional soil.

Step 3. Add compost. Spread 4–6 inches of compost across the entire area to be planted. No peat moss, pine bark, concrete sand, sandy loam, or artificial fertilizer should be used.

Step 4. Add rock minerals. Lava sand is my favorite and seems to be the most powerful, but other good choices include glacial rock powder, granite sand, greensand, zeolite, and colloidal (soft rock) phosphate. Apply to beds at 30–40 pounds per 1,000 square feet.

Step 5. Add fertilizer. Broadcast a 100 percent organic fertilizer onto the planting beds prior to tilling. Between 10 and 20 pounds per 1,000 square feet is enough. An application of a liquid biostimulant at label rates is also beneficial. An alternative is a tablespoon per gallon of natural apple cider vinegar and blackstrap molasses or sugar for a good homemade biostimulant.

Step 6. Mix compost and native soil together. Mix the compost and the existing topsoil together to a depth of about 10 inches, since most of the root activity of any plant will be in the top 6 to 9 inches of the soil. Never till deeper than 12 inches. Groundcover beds do not have to be tilled any deeper than 6–8 inches.

Step 7. Raise the beds. The finished grade of the beds should be flat on top, higher than the surrounding grades, and with sloped edges for good drainage. A raised effect will happen naturally as a result of tilling and the addition of air and compost. Leave a slight ditch around the edge of the bed to serve as a drainageway.

Step 8. Moisten beds before planting. Planting beds should be lightly watered before the planting begins. Do not install plants, especially small ones, in dry soil. This is critical during the hotter months, since dry soil can quickly dehydrate and kill tender roots.

Step 9. Set the plants properly. The top of the root ball should be level with the existing surrounding soil; plants set too low can easily drown, while planting too high can cause the upper roots to dry out. Natural root development is accelerated by spraying or soaking the roots of new plants with a biostimulant solution before they are planted. If they are tightly root-bound, be sure to tear or cut the roots to prevent later self-damage.

Step 10. Mulch the bare soil. The final planting step is to lay a 3–5-inch layer of organic mulch on the soil around new plants after planting. I use shredded hardwood bark or shredded native wood chips for shrubs and groundcovers, but I prefer rough-textured compost for annuals and perennials.

New plantings will establish and grow surprisingly well, and will be much easier to maintain, with this organic bed preparation.

Mulch, Mulch, Mulch!

I have a very important tip—mulch all bare soil. No—wait a minute, not a thin little amount of pine-bark mulch—use *real* mulch. Thick mulch. Mulch is not a soil amendment mixed into the soil; it's a covering, a blanket, a layer placed on top of the finished planting bed after the plants have been installed. Bare ground showing around trees, shrubs, groundcovers, flowers, or vegetables should be covered with at least 3 inches of mulch. This goes for both newly planted and existing plants.

While any natural mulch is better than no mulch at all, mulches vary in quality and effectiveness. I discovered through my own home-composting impatience that one of the best top-dressing mulches is partially completed compost. Not-quite-finished compost has a coarser texture and does a good job of letting air breathe through to the soil surface.

A good way to make your own "soon-to-be-mulch" compost pile is to form the three walls of the compost container with stacked hay bales. The size of the container can be as large or as small as you wish. Keep the hay-bale sides and the waste contents moist and turn the contents as often as you are able. After a few months the container and contents can be mixed together to create a nice big pile of wonderful mulch.

Grass clippings make a decent mulch if mixed with coarser debris such as leaves. I don't recommend using only lawn-grass clippings because the flat blades seal off the exchange of oxygen and carbon dioxide and create stinky, anaerobic conditions. The best mulch for use in the vegetable garden is thick and loose—straw and hay are excellent mulch material in this regard, even though they are coarse in appearance. Alfalfa is the best hay mulch because of its nutrient value and the presence of triacontanol, a growth regulator.

Another excellent mulch is shredded hardwood bark—tree bark from the lumber industry that has been run through a hammer mill. This smashing action gives the bark a fibrous texture that holds it in place even on sloping beds yet still allows air to circulate down to the soil. It's also a good-looking material.

Even though pine bark is still widely used as a mulch, fine to medium grades of pine bark make, at best, a second-rate mulch. If the pine bark doesn't blow or wash away, the flat pieces plate together and seal off the oxygen from the soil. Tars and resins in pine bark can also hinder proper aerobic degradation. Large, nugget-sized pine bark makes a fairly decent mulch because it will at least hold in place well, and since large nuggets don't fit together tightly, air can still circulate around them and get down to the soil.

While they shouldn't be mixed into the soil, fresh pine needles are excellent as a top-dressing mulch. Pine needles and other forest-floor debris make an especially effective mulch, when used in parts of the country where pine trees are native. Using material that is locally available and can be gathered from the forest floor is also economically advantageous, although moderation should be used to avoid causing a serious depletion of the organic matter in any natural setting.

Another good mulch for large areas is provided by tree chips. A by-product of the tree-care industry, tree chips are made from pruned limbs that are ground into chips. Although they are coarse in texture and often quite green, they make a good natural-looking mulch, especially after they have aged and become gray in color. Some tree-chipping machines can smash and grind tree chips into a finer texture. The resulting product makes an excellent top-dressing mulch, containing, as it does, buds, bits of leaves, and the cambium layer of branches and twigs, all of which are rich in protein and, therefore, nitrogen, since protein is 16 percent nitrogen.

I'm often asked whether sawdust or shavings make a good mulch. I don't recommend these materials unless they have been mixed with coarser materials and composted for a while (sawdust is an excellent ingredient for the compost pile). Pecan and other nut shells make a good top-dressing mulch, but they, too, are much better if composted first with other raw materials. Shredded cypress, although more expensive than most other mulches, is another fairly good mulch, but it tends to mat and seal off oxygen a little more than I would like, and it breaks down very slowly.

Groundcovers and new shrubs should be mulched with a coarse material that allows oxygen to circulate around the pieces and down to the surface of the soil. Large-sized pieces of decorative bark or tree chips are ideal. Put a light application of compost (½ inch or so) on the soil first and spread the coarse mulch on top. This technique duplicates a natural "forest-floor" profile and prevents the raw bark or chips from robbing nitrogen from the soil.

For newly planted trees, the top of the root ball should be

mulched with compost. Trees should be mulched whether planted in planting beds or in grass. When grass is planted over the top of the root ball, the oxygen is blocked from reaching the young feeder roots of the new tree.

I do not recommend artificial mulches such as those made from plastics and fabrics; they create artificial barriers to nature's systems. In fact, I don't recommend any nonorganic mulches— they don't biodegrade or return anything to the soil (although gravel, in general a lousy mulch, works well in utility areas). Natural mulches, in contrast, when applied in appropriately thick layers, will shade out weeds, eliminate the need to culti- vate, eliminate soil compaction, preserve soil moisture, main- tain the ideal soil temperature, and preserve and stimulate soil microorganisms.

Every gardening book you read will espouse the importance of mulch, but in real life, few people actually follow the advice. There's a fascinating test, however, originally run by Malcolm Beck in San Antonio, that can be conducted at home to prove the value of mulch and to serve as a reminder of how important it is to keep the soil cool and moist. During the summer, put a 4-inch depth of tree-chip mulch on an area of bare soil and leave an area nearby bare. The ground temperature readings 1 inch below the surface during a 100° F degree day will be startling. The tempera- ture of the soil under the mulch will be about 85°, whereas that of the soil outside the mulched area will be over 120°.

To follow up on the experiment, Malcolm checked the tem- perature during cooler parts of the day. The soil under the mulch was 83° F during a 97° afternoon and 78° at daybreak. Ideal soil temperature is 78–85°, while 120° will fry tender roots of plants. Proper temperature is important to other life in the soil as well. The protection of earthworms and microorganisms by maintaining soil temperature is the most important function of mulching.

Mulch can also reduce water bills by 30–50 percent, since it will keep the moisture level high in the mulched area for much longer. Mulch is important for many other reasons, too. For instance, it will stop erosion, eliminate weeds, regulate microbial and earthworm activity, and give beds a more finished look.

Don't fall into the trap of omitting the mulch at the end of the project in order to save a few bucks. Mulch is an excellent investment and one of the most important horticultural practices.

The Value of Aeration

If you are an organic gardener or ready to become one, it's time to go to work. And Step One is aeration. If I could get new organic gardeners to do just one thing differently, it would be to get more air in the ground. The value of aeration is greatly underestimated. Air is lacking in most soils, and punching holes in the ground or rototilling—the most common techniques of aeration—opens holes in the soil and allows nature's oxygen and other nutrients in the air to come in contact with the roots of plants.

It's a common misconception that nitrogen, phosphorus, and potassium (otherwise known as N-P-K) are the three most important elements for plants. The guy originally responsible for this error was Justus Von Liebig, a German scientist. Unfortunately this declaration that N-P-K are the most important elements has stuck and has been a major contributor to the overfertilizing of agricultural and landscape soils. By law, the percentage of nitrogen, phosphorus, and potassium has to be printed on each bag of fertilizer, which has to contain a guaranteed minimum of each of these three elements.

My point here is that in an organic program, the N-P-K ratio is practically irrelevant. The elements hydrogen, oxygen, and carbon (H-O-C) are much more important to the soil. These elements are readily available from the environment in the form of water, air, and organic matter; they are available, that is, in an organic program. Mechanical aeration simply speeds up this natural process of aeration.

Oxygen is a critical nutrient, but it's not the only important constituent of air. Air also contains carbon dioxide and nitrogen, both essential to soil and plant health, in large quantities, and many other mineral elements, such as copper, boron, iron, and sulfur, in small quantities. These nutrients are available to plant roots and microorganisms if there is enough pore space in the soil. The most noticeable response is to oxygen, which stimulates microbial activity and helps make other soil nutrients available to plant roots. Good aeration gives the same greening effect as that obtained by applying nitrogen fertilizer to the ground. The tall green grass around fire-ant mounds is primarily due to aeration by the ants in the ground.

Homeowners and commercial property owners can greatly improve the condition of their landscaping by helping hydrogen, oxygen, and carbon get into the top 6 inches of the soil. The process of mechanical aeration greatly benefits virtually all soils, especially clay soils, since the holes punched into the ground allow water and organic matter to penetrate into the root zone rather than rest on the surface to drain away or be oxidized into the air.

In addition, the holes provide the equally important service of allowing air to circulate more easily and further down into the root zone of lawn grasses, trees and shrubs, and other plants. Aeration will produce a new vigor in plants through increased root development and will provide a greening effect as though a high-nitrogen fertilizer had been applied.

If the soil conditions are right, all biological systems will work according to nature's plan. Soil that is open, well drained, rich in organic material, and moist will be loaded with microorganisms. These microscopic plants and animals feed on organic matter and minerals to create humus, humic acid, nitrogen, phosphorus, potassium, and other trace elements which are often locked up in the soil, significantly reducing the need to add high levels of traditional fertilizer nutrients. Working with nature's systems in this way not only will increase the health of the plants but also will effect a significant cost savings over the long haul. Mechanical aeration is possibly the most significant single procedure to use on your soil—especially when converting to organics from the unhealthy condition of chemical dependency.

Soil will naturally become aerated by the addition of organic matter and the stimulation of microbial activity if given enough time. All you have to do for nature to take its course is add compost and organic fertilizers and stop using harsh, synthetic products. However, most of us want the process to go faster, and in that case, the answer is to punch holes in the ground. These holes, rips, or tears can be punched with a stiff-tined turning fork, or with any spiked tool. The most convenient method is to buy or rent a mechanical aerator or hire a landscape contractor to use one to poke holes or slice cuts all over the yard. Hand work usually has to be done in the beds.

Mechanical aerators are available in many shapes and sizes, and with a variety of features. Some just punch small holes, while others cut slits, remove cores, or inject water while punching holes; some can even punch holes 12 inches deep. All of these machines do the job, though the more penetration, the better. Just choose a machine that fits your budget, because the cost varies greatly. I have used machines made by Bluebird, Toro, Ryan, and Aer-Way, and even some home-made machines; they all work. The object is to get oxygen into the soil. When that happens, microbe populations increase, natural nitrogen cycles function properly, and nature's wonderful systems are all set in motion. It's not necessary to understand all the systems in great detail—it's only important to respect their presence and let them work for you.

Re-creating the Forest Floor

Here's an easy way to understand how to become organic: Re-create the forest floor in all your beds—in your vegetable gardens, orchards, herb gardens, rose gardens, and other ornamental gardens.

A natural forest-floor cross-section looks like this: the top 2–4 inches consist of mulch—leaves, twigs, bark, dead plants, dead bodies of animals, and animal manure. Below that are 1–2 inches of one-year-old organic matter which is well broken down into humus. Next is a mixture of humus and the rock dust of the area (broken-up pieces of the base rock material in which the minerals are contained). Below that is the subsoil. Earthworms, insects, microbes, and roots are all mixed throughout the layers. The top 7 inches of the forest floor is the area that is the best aerated and that contains the largest percentage of microscopic plants and animals.

This very definite layering of rough mulch on top of humus and native soil is nature's way of covering, protecting, and stimulating the soil. Why, then, should we not do the same thing in our cultivated gardens? Nowhere in the wild will nature allow the ground to be bare (nowhere, that is, apart from natural desert areas and naturally eroded areas around rivers and above the frost lines of mountains). It is that same layered structure, then, graduated from rough mulch on the top to subsoil beneath, that we want to create in the vegetable garden and in the ornamental garden.

There are several ways to re-create the forest floor in the garden. The easiest way is to take the leaves from your own property or from the plastic bags neighbors have left along the street and dump them onto bare areas in the planting beds. The depth of this raw material can range from 8 to 12 inches. This easy method can also be used with hay, tree chips, or virtually any raw organic material. Fine-textured matter such as sawdust, if used at all, should be applied in thinner layers, since there is less air space between the small pieces and therefore less exchange of oxygen and carbon dioxide at the soil surface. It's better, however, to compost such fine-textured materials before using them in the beds.

A better way to re-create the forest floor is to use partially finished compost (that is, compost in which a portion of the raw materials can still be identified). The texture of the material will be better, because a mix of large, small, and decomposed particles will exist, and soil improvement will be faster, because of the large quantity of beneficial microorganisms present. I use partially completed compost as mulch at a depth of 6–8 inches.

To go a step farther, apply a layer of finished compost on the bare soil at a depth of 1–2 inches and cover it with a 3–6-inch-thick blanket of any of the coarse-textured materials mentioned above; alternatively, use hardwood bark, pine needles, cypress mulch, or hay. Pine bark can be used, but it is not ideal because its flat pieces can plate together to seal off oxygen, and it can be moved around easily by wind and water. Likewise, I do not recommend using mulches made from paper, plastic, or gravel, unless you have no source of vegetative materials.

Covering the bare soil with mulch is probably the single most important aspect of organic gardening, and various mulching methods will work to keep the soil temperature and moisture level correct, prevent wind and water erosion, and stimulate the life in the soil. If I could choose an ideal mulch with which to recreate the forest floor, it would be this:

Step 1. Spray bare soil with fish emulsion, seaweed, and natural vinegar or some other biostimulant. Mix one or more of these materials at 1 tablespoon per gallon of water.

Step 2. Till 4–6 inches of compost into the native soil. If tree roots exist, do this by hand, not with a tiller.

Step 3. Apply a light coating of earthworm castings—just enough to barely cover the soil.

Step 4. Apply a ½-inch layer of finished compost.

Step 5. Apply a 1-inch layer of partially finished compost.

Step 6. Apply a 2-inch layer of hardwood bark mulch or shredded native tree chips.

Note: As a precaution, don't pile the mulch up onto the trunks of trees. If the mulch is kept constantly wet, it can cause the trunk to rot.

If that sounds like a lot of trouble, it is. That's why I gave you the other choices above.

Don't Bag Those Leaves

When the leaves fall to the ground, having completed their summer job of making food from sunlight, it's time for them to start their second job. Although to many homeowners, leaves on the ground are a nuisance and only represent work, they are actually a great resource and asset at this stage—one which we simply have to understand how to use.

Dead leaves are nature's way of fertilizing the ground. Everything in nature is recycled—nothing is ever wasted—and the fallen leaves, combined with the bodies and manure of insects and other animals, are all that nature uses to fertilize the soil. The value of leaves as a fertilizer lies not only in the fact that they provide organic matter and humus; in addition, they have a very high mineral content—in fact, they contain more mineral nutrients than does the same weight of manure. They contain calcium, magnesium, potash, phosphorus, nitrogen, and many trace elements. Thus, sending plastic bags of organic matter to the city dump is tantamount to throwing fertilizer away.

Leaves can be left right where they fall. Some folks don't think this approach looks right, especially on the lawn, because the leaves cover up too much of the landscaping. In that case, the leaves can be blown or raked off the lawn into the planting beds. This works best after they have been shredded, since grinding the leaves into a finer texture makes them easier to handle and speeds up their decomposition by increasing the surface area for the microorganisms to feed on. There are various ways to shred the leaves. Rotary mowers can be used to mulch them before putting them in the beds. A mulching mower or attachment for your traditional mower makes the process even more efficient, but it's not absolutely necessary. Still another method is to pile the leaves in a thick layer on the driveway and drive over them several times.

Another option is to use the leaves, as a soil amendment or a top-dressing mulch, after they have been rotted in the compost pile. Since leaves have a very high carbon content, a nitrogen source is needed for the leaves to break down quickly. Use 2 cups of blood meal or bat guano per wheelbarrow load of leaves or a 1:5 ratio of manure to leaves and other vegetative material. A 1 percent fish-emulsion solution (2½ tablespoons per gallon of water) can be used as an additional nitrogen source. Wet the foliage while mixing in this material, since it's very difficult to wet leaves or other organic materials thoroughly once they are in the compost pile.

I am often asked which kinds of leaves can be used in the compost pile. The most frequent questions concern oak, pecan, walnut, and sycamore leaves. The answer is that all leaves are a good source of organic matter and make good compost ingredients. Even though walnut and sycamore leaves do contain growth inhibitors, the composting process eliminates the problem. I do not recommend tilling raw leaves into the ground unless done in the fall, allowing the material to compost in the ground over the winter before the planting is done in the spring.

Bags of leaves and vegetative debris that uninformed neighbors are still sending to the landfills can and should be used in the garden. My favorite way of using such neighbor-provided material is to throw it into the compost pile and let the natural biodegradation break down any pesticide residues.

All of the weeds and spent annuals, perennials, and vegetables should be added to the compost pile and mixed with the leaves and manure. If you don't own a shredder, a good way to grind them up is to use an old chopping block, or just a large board, and a machete to chop the material into small pieces. Even though there is some effort involved in all this leaf business, you will find it has been worthwhile when you see the soil improvement and related plant growth. And in addition, it's all good exercise.

Mineralization

Mineralization is one of those words that organiphobes try to ignore and avoid. It refers to the balance of chemical nutrients in the soil. These include calcium, magnesium, potassium, phosphorus, sulfur, sodium, and trace minerals such as aluminum, argon, boron, cobalt, copper, gold, iron, manganese, silicon, silver, and zinc. It's a fact of life that in the last fifty years, synthetic agriculture and landscape programs have reduced the amount of nutrients stored in the soil. When farmers refer to worn-out farms, what's worn out is the soil. Even land with healthy soil can be quickly depleted if organic matter and minerals are not recycled back into the ground to make up for their depletion when the harvested crops are taken from the land. That depletion can be stopped. With proper management, remineralization can occur.

First, we need to stop mining the soil. Some of the nutrients stored in plants come from the air, but a larger percentage comes from the soil. When plant residue is sent to the landfill, the minerals go with it. The demineralization of grasslands, landscapes, and lawns can be stopped simply by leaving the clippings on the ground. Don't sell the hay off and don't bag the clippings.

After we have stopped mining the soil, the healing process can begin by adding nutrients back to it. Compost is always the first choice because it adds minerals as well as organic matter and humus. Granular organic fertilizers, however, offer the same ingredients and can be applied more easily with conventional fertilizer spreaders.

To speed up the process further, there are several other mineral choices. Although significant research has just begun to show which products are best, here are some general guidelines.

Colloidal phosphate. Colloidal phosphate (also called soft rock phosphate) is a mixture of fine particles of phosphate suspended in a clay base. It is an economical form of natural phosphorus and calcium. Unlike chemically made phosphates, natural phosphate is insoluble in water, will not leach away, and therefore, is long lasting. It contains 18 percent phosphorus and 15 percent calcium as well as many trace elements. Florida is the primary source. Hard rock phosphate is a less soluble form of natural phosphorus, simply because the pieces of rock are larger.

Granite sand. Granite sand is a residue from the granite quarry or from natural deposits of weathered granite. It provides an excellent way to add slow-release minerals to planting beds, lawns, and fields, and is a much better choice than washed concrete sand, as well as an excellent source of potash (potassium).

Greensand. Greensand (glauconite) is often sold as Jersey greensand. It is an iron potassium silicate that is naturally deposited in the sea. An excellent source of potash and all trace minerals, it is best used with other fertilizers and is a good potting-soil ingredient.

Limestone. Lime is a major calcium fertilizer. High-calcium lime which contains only 10 percent magnesium is preferred over the more commonly sold dolomitic lime, or dolomite, because low-calcium soils usually contain too much magnesium. Dolomite is approximately 30 percent magnesium and is not the best choice for moving the soil chemistry toward balance.

Lava. Lava sand is the waste material from lava gravel. It is an excellent, high-energy soil-amendment material loaded with minute amounts of many trace minerals, and will improve any soil.

Humate. This geologic term refers to a naturally occurring, highly compressed, highly decomposed organic material. It includes a very broad spectrum of organic fractions, including RNA, DNA, humic substances, auxins, polypeptides, trace minerals, and other organic (carbon-based) compounds.

Sul-Po-Mag. Sul-Po-Mag, or langbeinite, contains 22 percent sulfur, 22 percent potash, and 11 percent magnesium, and is a natural source of these elements.

Zeolite. Zeolite is a natural hydrated silicate of aluminum and either sodium or calcium. Artificial zeolites also exist. Both are used as detergent builders for water softening, as absorbents, as desiccants, and as deodorants for livestock stalls, pets' areas, and shoes. Zeolite is also an excellent natural kitty litter. In the soil, zeolite acts as a slow-release mechanism for moisture, potassium, and ammonium and reduces the leaching of nutrients caused by heavy rainfall or irrigation.

Each of these natural materials contains a blend of many trace minerals. Some, as noted, have a more balanced blend than others. Those that are heavy in certain mineral nutrients can be used to help correct severe deficiencies. For those who don't want to take a college course in chemistry to learn how to balance the minerals in the soil, here's an easy way to remineralize it:

1. Recycle heavy amounts of organic matter back into the soil by leaving the clippings on the ground, and regularly apply compost, organic fertilizers, and mulch to beds.

2. Apply greensand or lava sand to all planting beds at the rate of 20–80 pounds per 1,000 square feet.

3. Apply granulated Sul-Po-Mag to alkaline soils at 20 pounds per 1,000 square feet, or apply high-calcium lime to acid soils at 40 pounds per 1,000 square feet.

4. Spray foliage monthly during the growing season with fish emulsion, liquid seaweed, blackstrap molasses, and natural apple cider vinegar, each at 1 tablespoon per gallon of water.

Feed the Soil—Not the Plants

Many in the gardening world are now switching to organic fertilizers. Great results are being seen, but a lot of folks are still reluctant to change because they don't have a clear understanding of how organic fertilizers work and why artificial fertilizers are a problem.

One of the sources of misunderstanding lies in the fact that organic fertilizers appear to have low levels of the elements we hear about most often—namely, nitrogen, phosphorus, and potassium (N-P-K), which are by far the most commonly recommended nutrients. For example, the recommended analysis in Texas for thirty years or more has been a 3-1-2 ratio fertilizer, such as 15-5-10 (i.e., 15 percent nitrogen, 5 percent phosphorus, and 10 percent potash). Although that's changing now to a 1-0-0 analysis, which is a move in the right direction, there's more to understanding how to fertilize. The main idea behind the 1-0-0 ratio fertilizer is that potassium and phosphorus are not needed, since these elements already exist in large quantities in the soil. However, that theory overlooks the fact that although a soil test might show high levels of potassium and phosphorus, these nutrients might not be available to plants because of poor aeration, low humus, and general imbalance.

The fact is that plants need more than nitrogen, phosphorus, and potassium. It's likely that they need all 92 natural mineral elements, because an analysis of healthy plant tissue reveals traces of all 92 elements. And guess what? Most natural organic fertilizers contain all 92 elements. That's because these plant foods come from plants. Even if the fertilizer is animal manure, the cow first ate grass or the chicken ate grain—you see my point. The famous elements N-P-K are important, but so are carbon, hydrogen, oxygen, sulfur, magnesium, copper, cobalt, sodium, boron, molybdenum, and zinc, to name but a few. These minerals are all present in composted manure fertilizers such as Sustane, Gro Up, GreenSense, Garden-Ville Soil Food, Living Earth, Ringer, and Maestro Gro. A balance of all the necessary mineral nutrients is also present in meals, such as alfalfa, cottonseed, soybean, and fish meal. Fish meal and cottonseed meal should be used sparingly—they are very powerful and can burn plants or shut down nature's systems if overused. For beginning organic gardeners, fertilizer should be applied first in early spring, at 20 pounds per 1,000 square feet, and then again in June at the same rate. To push things along a little faster, a third application can be made in September. Timing is not that critical with organic fertilizers.

Earthworm castings show how unimportant high N-P-K numbers are. Possibly nature's most perfectly balanced and most effective fertilizer, they have an analysis of less than 1-1-1. Some organic contractors use nothing but this product, and their gardens are always green and beautiful and the flowers showy. Compost, nature's own fertilizer, usually has an analysis of around 1-1-1.

What's wrong with synthetic fertilizers? They contain no carbon, no organic matter, and few, if any, trace minerals. They often contain high levels of nitrates and other salts, which can inhibit or destroy beneficial soil microorganisms. They usually work too fast and can glut plants with excessive amounts of nutrients—especially nitrogen. Nitrogen glut leads to thin cell walls and greater susceptibility to insect and pathogen attack, as well as a lessened ability to withstand drought, cold, and salt effects.

Eating too much processed sugar creates the same nutrient imbalance in humans. To metabolize the sugar, minerals and vitamins must be borrowed from the body, leaving it more susceptible to colds, flu, and more serious diseases.

How does the plant get enough nitrogen? Nitrogen is plentiful in a properly functioning natural system—the air is almost 80 percent nitrogen. Certain microbes in the soil can grab nitrogen right out of the air in the soil, which is why aeration is so important. Nitrogen is also released in the soil by microorganisms feeding on organic matter. That's why compost is so important and why I recommend it so highly over all other forms of organic matter.

How Organic Programs Save Water

During my preorganic days in the early 1970s, I lived for several years in the Lakewood area of East Dallas, where the soil was black clay on top of white rock. The rock was fractured and the drainage was quite good—so good, in fact, that either my wife or I had to water every day to keep the new planting from wilting. In those days our irrigation was done by standing at the end of a water hose. As a result, water bills were high, and we almost divorced over whose turn it was to water and whose fault it was that the azaleas were wilted.

Although I didn't realize it at the time, I was having to water too much because my maintenance program was chemical rather than organic. At this point, both in my career as a landscape architect and as a home gardener, I did not realize how important it was to use compost for bed preparation, to mulch the top of planted beds, and to fertilize with organic products. And I certainly didn't realize that with every application of synthetic fertilizer and chemical pesticide, I was killing a few hundred thousand or more living organisms in the soil and on my plants.

Of all the pleasant surprises resulting from my organic education, one of the most important has been the water-savings aspect. Organic programs save water in the following way. Healthy soil that is high in organic matter and microorganisms holds more moisture. The organic material itself absorbs and holds water, but that's not the only reason. Increased organic levels provide the necessary food and energy supply for the microorganisms to multiply and exist at a healthy level. Gluelike polysaccharides form and join the small clay particles together to create larger soil particles and air spaces between the particles that allow water, oxygen, and nutrients to penetrate the soil easily. My chemically maintained soil wasn't accepting the water, and much was being wasted as runoff. Unhealthy soil can repel water like a duck's back. Healthy soil accepts water easily and drains well, but here's the secret—it holds a healthy level of moisture for a longer period of time. Even sandy soils that drain too fast are helped by the addition of organic matter, rock minerals, and living organisms. In sand, the water percolation is slowed down and the soil again holds an appropriate level of moisture. Magic! When moisture remains in the soil at an appropriately healthy level, less irrigation is needed, water bills go down, and plant production goes up.

Additional savings can be realized by adjusting the watering schedule. It's best to water less often, more deeply, and longer at each watering. No one schedule works for everyone, but start by watering two times per week for thirty minutes each time and adjust from there. Many mature gardens can get away with one deep watering per week or even less.

Remember how important it is to leave the clippings on the lawn; and as a final water-saving measure, raise the cutting height of your mower—most common grasses should be mowed at 2½–3 inches. Cutting the grass higher looks good, reduces the stress caused by mowing, and helps to shade the soil, which both reduces weed-seed germination and helps soil moisture to be retained longer.

3 Fertilization

Compost—Mother Nature's Fertilizer

Some of the most common questions I get asked through my newspaper column and radio show have to do with building and managing a compost pile. *What is compost? What should go in the pile? How do you mix the ingredients? Is compost a fertilizer? How do I use compost? How big does the pile need to be? Why won't my compost heat up? Why won't my compost rot? What is the white stuff in my compost? How do I get rid of the insects in my compost? Why does my compost stink?*

The simple definition of compost is organic matter that's broken down into an unidentifiable form. Every living thing on earth is going to die, and everything that dies, rots. Completely rotted material is compost. Compost contains many nutrients and therefore is a fertilizer—the best fertilizer on earth, since it's nature's own. Composting is also an excellent organic process for recycling waste—a bad term to use for organic matter, which is an important natural resource, not a waste by-product.

Compost comes from the Latin word for "bring together." I like composts that are made from several different ingredients. The ideal mixture is 75–80 percent dry, brown vegetative matter and 20–25 percent animal manure and green plant material. The best composting materials are those that exist on your own property; next best are those that are easily obtainable nearby. The locations of the compost pile can be in sun or shade, and covers are not necessary (although some composters like to use covers to prevent rains from cooling the pile).

There are many good recipes for compost, but it's almost impossible to foul up the compost-making process. Even 100 percent pure vegetative matter or animal matter can be composted. Composting is as much an art as a science, and a little experimenting is good. I find that the simplest systems are usually the best. With new gardens or planting beds, the composting can be done in the beds by lightly tilling raw organic matter into the soil. Once this has been done, it's best to wait at least two months to plant. Surface composting, like the composting on a forest floor, simply takes a little longer than composting in a pile.

Composting should be done whenever the raw materials are available, and compost piles should be working year round. A convenient site, such as a utility area behind the garage or a dog run, should be chosen for the location of the compost pile, and for greatest efficiency, it should be on a paved surface so that the leachate can be caught and used as a liquid fertilizer. The advantage of locating a compost pile on soil, however, is that although the leachate is wasted, the earthworms can enter the pile easily and help complete the composting process.

Should I use a container and if so what kind? I personally don't use a container at all—I just pile the material on the ground or in the dog run or driveway. Some people, however, want to be neat, while others think using a container makes better compost, and some just like to buy and build gadgets. Whatever the reason, if you need to use a container, compost bins can be made out of wooden pallets, wood frame with wire mesh, corrugated tin, plastic, fiberglass, hay bales, old signs, old tires, cinder blocks, untreated lumber, or whatever else you have lying around that has a minimum volume of 3 cubic feet. Avoid chemically treated wood, especially railroad ties, since the heavy metals in the preservative are highly toxic to both tiny and large living organisms. Store-bought compost bins are also available; they're hardly worth the cost, but it's your money. Just make sure you have plenty of space—although if you have the space, a container isn't really even necessary—just make a big pile. Even apartment dwellers, however, can make compost at home; containers made from plastic, rubber, fiberglass, and other recycled materials make excellent compost bins for people with limited space.

Hay bales make good natural building blocks to form a compost container. Stack the bales to make a two- or three-sided enclosure. The hay bales can ultimately be pulled into the mix to become part of the compost.

Good compost ingredients include grass clippings, leaves of all kinds, sawdust, dead plants, weeds (and no, don't worry about the weed seeds), tree chips, coffee grounds, tea leaves, feathers, old bird seed, feather meal, seaweed, peanut hulls, pine cones, pecan hulls and other nut shells, fish scraps, brewery waste, slaughter-house waste, pine needles, wool, silk, cotton, granite dust, uncooked vegetable scraps, fruit peelings, pet hair, dust, and animal manure. Some say dog and cat manure should not be used in the compost pile. I don't have cats, but I do use my dogs' manure in the piles, since a properly managed compost pile will neutralize almost all pathogens. Make your own decision on this point. It's best to avoid greasy or cooked foods, newspaper or other dyed or printed materials, synthetic fabrics, burned charcoal, and plastics.

Compost materials should be chopped or ground into pieces of different sizes and thoroughly mixed together. Compost piles that contain uniform particles will not breathe properly. Although most books recommend adding the ingredients a layer at a time, it is unnecessary to do so unless it will help to get the correct proportions of vegetative material (carbon) and animal matter (nitrogen) at the outset. After the first turning, the layers won't be there anymore. Green plant material contains water and nitrogen and will break down faster than dry, brown, withered high-carbon materials. It's a good idea to add some native soil (a couple of shovels full) to each pile to inoculate it with native soil microorganisms. To thrive, microorganisms need an energy source (provided by any carbon material, such as leaves or wood), a nitrogen or food source (such as manure, green foliage, or organic fertilizers), and vitamins (stored in most living tissue).

Moisture is a critical ingredient in the compost pile. Watering the pile thoroughly while mixing the raw ingredients is the best way to ensure sufficient moisture content—between 40 and 50 percent, similar to the wetness of a squeezed-out sponge. Piles that are too wet will be anaerobic (lacking air), and piles that are too dry won't compost properly either. Once the pile is evenly moist, it's easy to maintain. Add a little water during dry periods, and turn it more often during rainy spells. If there are ants in your compost pile, it's usually because it's too dry. If it smells bad, it's usually too wet or has too much nitrogen, in which case add some carbon material such as dry leaves, sawdust, or wood chips. The presence of white fungus in the pile is beneficial; this is actinomycetes, the fungus that helps break down organic matter and gives the compost its fresh, forest-floor smell.

Turning the compost mixes air throughout the material and ensures that all the ingredients are exposed to the cleaning heat of beneficial fungi, bacteria, and other microorganisms that are working to break the raw material down into humus. A properly "cooking" compost pile, with a heat of approximately 140–160° will kill the weed seeds and harmful pathogens but will stimulate the beneficial microorganisms. Don't be concerned if your pile heats for a while and then cools off—that's natural. The entire process takes anywhere from two months to a year, depending on how often the pile is turned. If the ingredients contain a high percentage of wood chips or bamboo, the process may take even longer. Counterintuitively, softwood sawdust or chips break down slower than hardwood.

Turn or stir the pile at least once a month, but preferably every two weeks, or even weekly. While turning it daily will speed up the process the most, if you have time to turn the pile daily, you should seriously think about getting a life! Besides, frequent turning causes lots of the nitrogen to be wasted by gassing off. Large commercial piles are turned about four times in seven months.

Use biological activators to speed up the process. Several compost-starter products claim to stimulate microbes and make the pile heat up and cook faster. Good store-bought materials are available from Agrispon, Agri-Gro, Garden-Ville, Nitron, Medina, Bioform, Ringer, and Necessary Trading Company. If the budget allows, go ahead and use one of them—they won't hurt, and they might even help. However, you do have some microbe stimulators at home already. Molasses, for example—especially dry molasses—is an excellent compost accelerator, and other biostimulants include sugar, syrup, native soil, and finished compost, as well as any organic fertilizer. Liquid fish emulsion is also very effective. Do you *have* to use any of these things? Nope. Not if you build the pile originally with about 75 percent vegetable matter and 25 percent manure. As I've already said, compost can be made purely from either vegetative materials or manure, but the best mix is 75–80 percent dry brown stuff and 20–25 percent green stuff, manure, or organic fertilizers.

Compost has many uses. Unfinished compost makes a very effective top-dressing mulch for ornamental beds and vegetable gardens. Compost is finished and ready to use as a fertilizer and soil amendment when the original material is no longer identifiable, the texture is soft and crumbly, and the fragrance is rich and earthy.

Compost is an excellent natural fertilizer for grass areas, planting beds, vegetable gardens, and potted plants. It is the only organic material needed for new bed preparation. The fact that it's alive makes it better than pine bark or peat moss, and in addition, it has many nutrients, whereas peat moss doesn't. All gardeners should make at least some of their own compost even if they have to supplement it with commercially made products.

The following are some of the most commonly asked compost questions.

Will the compost pile stink? No, not if you keep it aerated.

Compost piles that stink don't have enough air. Either they are anaerobic or they contain too much concentrated nitrogen material. To stop the stink, add dry carbonaceous material. *Carbonaceous*—isn't that a nice word? It means brown stuff—dry leaves, sawdust, dead plants, and so forth. Simply turning the pile will often end the stink, but the brown materials will absorb the ammonia gas and help balance the mixture so that the odor won't return.

I'm handicapped, too old, too tired, or too lazy to turn the pile—what am I to do? Well, you need to build your pile a little differently. Lay a perforated (full of holes) PVC (plastic) pipe on the ground and pile the material on top of it, leaving the ends of the pipe sticking out from the sides of the pile. Some folks like to stand the pipe up in the middle of the pile. That's okay, too. Do both if it makes you feel good. With this method, no turning is necessary. The only drawback is that the material on the outside of the pile won't get the purifying heat of the interior. A few weed seeds might germinate; if they do, pull them out.

Should I put dog and cat poop in the pile? As I mentioned earlier, I use dog manure in my compost pile, but not cat manure, because I don't have any cats. Some people are afraid of cat manure because of a pathogen that is supposedly dangerous, especially for pregnant women. However, properly composted material is pathogen free. It's your choice.

How do I control fire ants and grubs in the pile? Turn the pile more often, or add cottonseed meal or some other nitrogen source to heat things up. Dry molasses is also a good choice. If the grubs are as big as your thumb, don't do anything—that's the rhinoceros beetle, a good bug.

Do I need to cover the pile? Only if it rains all the time—which I guess means yes, in parts of the country. Protecting the pile from supersaturation is the only reason to cover compost with a lid or tarp. The pros don't use covers on their big commercial piles.

My pile was hot for a while, but now it's cool. What happened? It's natural for the pile to cool after a while unless there is lots of nitrogen material in it. The forest floor composts the organic matter without any heat—and does a pretty good job, I might add.

When is the pile ready to use, and how do you use it? Partially finished compost can be used as an excellent top-dressing mulch. Finished compost is soft, sweet smelling, and formless. It should be mixed into the existing soil to prepare new beds, used as a high-quality top-dressing mulch, raked into aeration holes to improve any soil, or used as an excellent fertilizer on any plants—including potted plants—and on turf.

I hope this has helped you understand compost. If I had to choose only one fertilizer for my gardens, it would be compost, hands down.

Don't Compost Grass Clippings

Smart cities have decided to stop collecting grass clippings and to encourage homeowners and businesses to leave the clippings on the lawn. That's a good decision, but it has provoked some interesting complaints. *It costs too much! It causes thatch! It causes disease! Midnight dumping of clippings will start! Composting is too much trouble! I'm on a tight budget and can't afford to mow more often! I'm a senior citizen and can't manage a compost pile!* The list goes on . . .

Let me try to straighten all this out. Sit back and relax and let me explain a few things about grass maintenance and composting. There's so much bad information about how to handle natural resources, it's hard to decide where to start, but here goes.

Cities have decided to stop picking up grass clippings in order to save money—lots of money. Saving landfill space is not their most important consideration. Surprised? The real reason is that everyone, including homeowners, businesses, cities, states, and countries, can save money and improve the soil and turf by leaving the clippings on the lawn. Grass clippings make up at least 25 percent of the lawn's nutrient requirements. And no, leaving them doesn't cause thatch or disease; quite the contrary. It's not necessary to mow more often, either—once a week is plenty, as long as you also stop using high-nitrogen synthetic fertilizers. (Incidentally, it's these fertilizers that are recommended by the same people who recommend mowing every four or five days—it's a brilliant plan—spend more money to fertilize more often so you can mow more often . . . Makes sense to me!)

When natural organic fertilizers are used instead, nature's systems take care of most problems. Soil microorganisms feed on the clippings to prevent thatch, and the good microbes control the bad microbes, thus preventing disease.

Leaving the clippings on the ground is nothing but beneficial. It cuts mowing time by 40 percent, provides nutrients and food for microorganisms, makes the lawn look better, and saves everyone money.

Do I have to buy a new mower? You don't have to, but it helps, since mulching mowers do work better than non-mulching mowers to grind the grass into finer pieces. In fact, these machines are fantastic. If you have to buy a new mower anyway, don't consider anything but a mulching mower. Quality mulching mowers such as those made by Bolens, Honda, Snapper, and Troy-bilt will leave no unsightly residue, even after mowing tall grass. But you don't have to buy a new mower immediately. Mulching blades can be added to almost any mower, and regular old mowers that blow the clippings out the side will work without any modification—in fact, I mowed my own lawn for three years with a regular side-discharge mower, and didn't catch the clippings. Raking and removing excess clippings still took less time than emptying the bags every two minutes. Don't get me wrong, though; when you can afford a new mulching mower, get one. By the way, the grass is never too high to mow with a mulching mower. The idea that you need two mowers when using a mulcher comes from those who don't use organic fertilizers or who have never actually used a mulching mower.

Seaweed/Fish Emulsion and Foliar Feeding

My ultimate goal is to help you understand that if the soil is healthy and if you have selected good strong plants that are well adapted to your site, you won't even have to use organic insecticides like soapy water, pyrethrum, and diatomaceous earth. At least you won't need them very often. But for now, while I'm helping you make the transition from chemical to natural landscaping, here's another tip on controlling specific problems.

A mixture of liquid seaweed (kelp) and fish emulsion not only is a great fertilizer but also has some additional benefits that you will find quite helpful. First, though, let me say a word or two about both of these natural products.

Fish emulsion. This concentrated fertilizer can be used directly on the soil or as a foliar spray. The N-P-K analysis will range from 4-1-1 to 5-2-2, although in an organic program that doesn't mean much. It is a great all-purpose spray, especially when mixed with liquid seaweed and other products. Fish emulsion does stink about twenty-four hours after use—but then, so do many of the chemical products. Deodorizers are available. Molasses, at 1 tablespoon per gallon of water, acts as a natural deodorizer and provides trace minerals and carbohydrates at the same time.

Liquid seaweed. Kelp is an excellent source of trace minerals and is a good stimulator of microbial activity. It is most effective when used often in light doses. It contains hormones which stimulate root growth, branching, and cold tolerance. At least sixty trace elements are found in seaweed, and in the same proportions in which they are found in plants.

Liquid seaweed also works as a fertilizer through the foliage and through the soil, quickly giving green color to plants. One of the incorrect ideas about organics is that the results are slower. That's wrong. If the correct products are used at the right time of the year, the greening and growth of plants is surprisingly quick. Since seaweed is full of trace elements and has effective growth-regulating hormones, it acts as an excellent root stimulator. Use it when planting new trees. After digging a rough-sided hole, fill it with water, and then add seaweed to the water at the rate of about 1 ounce of seaweed per 5 gallons of water. Don't forget to backfill the natural way, using only the soil from the hole. Finish the planting procedure with ½–1 inch of good-quality compost on top of the root ball, followed by 3–5 inches of coarse mulch. Seaweed used in this way as a root stimulator helps get the new trees off to the best possible start.

Liquid seaweed also seems to have very definite fungicidal properties when sprayed on grass, ornamental plants, or fruit trees, as does fish emulsion; they can be used separately or mixed together. The mixing rate will vary from product to product, so check the label instructions carefully. The mixture does leave an odor for a while, but so do poisonous chemicals. To lessen the odor, omit the fish emulsion. A 50 percent fish emulsion and 50 percent seaweed mixture is an excellent all-purpose spray for foliar and soil feeding and for insect and fungus control. Even though the manufacturers are restricted from advertising some of these side benefits, I can tell you from personal experience that they work. And I'm not the only one; others in the business have also given strong testimony to the power of these products. An arborist from Chicago recently called me, after hearing about my involvement in organics, to tell me about his highly successful twenty-year-old organic tree-care business. When I asked him what products he used in his business, he had a simple answer— fish emulsion and seaweed.

Foliar feeding has been used since 1844, when it was discovered that plant nutrients could be leached out from the leaves by rain. Experiments soon proved that nutrients could also enter plants through the foliage. It's still somewhat of a mystery exactly how the nutrients enter the plant through the foliage, but it is known and undisputed that the process works, and that it works quickly. For something further to think about, there is also evidence that nutrients can be absorbed through the bark of trees.

The more I learn about soil, biology, horticulture, and organics, the more convinced I become about the importance of foliar feeding. Research related to foliar feeding has been available for some time; T. L. Senn of Clemson University wrote about it in detail in his book *Seaweed and Plant Growth*, in which he explained the wonderful powers of seaweed as a fertilizer and root stimulatoɪ and how to use foliar feeding to supplement a soil-fertilization program.

Foliar feeding is 300–400 times more efficient than soil fertilization, and organic foliar sprays are the most effective, since their nutrients are in a more balanced proportion for plant growth.

In addition to feeding, some spray products stimulate soil and plant systems. Agrispon, Medina, Bioform, and other biological products activate plant growth and flower/fruit production by increasing both photosynthesis in the foliage and the translocation of fluids and energy within the plant, as well as stimulating microorganisms in the soil and increasing the uptake of nutrients from the soil through the root hairs. Foliar feeding increases the efficiency of all the natural systems in the soil and in the plants, resulting in bigger, stronger, healthier plants with increased drought, insect, and disease resistance.

Here are some updated points to remember when using foliar sprays.

1. Less is usually better in foliar sprays—in other words, light, regularly applied sprays are better than heavy, infrequent blasts, and mists of liquid are better than big drops.

2. Young, tender foliage absorbs nutrients better than old, hard, mature foliage, so it's best to foliar feed during the periods of new growth on plants.

3. Sugar and molasses added to spray solutions can stimulate the growth of beneficial microorganisms on the leaf surfaces and in the soil. These friendly microbes help fight off the harmful pathogens. Whether this is provable or not is beside the point; just accept it—it works.

4. Spraying on damp, humid mornings or evenings increases the effectiveness of foliar sprays. The least effective time to foliar feed is during the heat of midday, since small openings in the leaves, called stomata, close up during the heat of the day or as a result of other stress so that moisture within the plant is preserved. The best time of day to spray is late afternoon unless it's still extremely hot; the next best time is early morning. Gases and liquids are best absorbed through the leaves during the after-

noon, because that's when the plant processes reverse, so that the fluids are moving down in the plant and root exudation is at its peak at that time of the day.

5. Well-timed foliar feeding on food crops will increase their storage life.

Other effective products and mixtures for foliar feeding include, but are certainly not limited to, the following:

Agrispon. This liquid biostimulant, made in Dallas, accelerates root growth and top growth. It helps to control harmful pathogens of all sorts through increased biological activity. It can be used on soil, foliage, and seed prior to planting. It will reduce a plant's drought and salt stress and increase the efficiency of all fertilizer elements, especially nitrogen.

Agri-Gro. This is a liquid that contains enzymes and living microorganisms. It provides increased growth, greater production, and higher quality of produce. It works best when mixed with blackstrap molasses.

Bioform. An excellent product, this is one of the best tools to use when converting from a chemical to an organic program. The fish emulsion it contains is made from whole fish, seaweed, molasses, and enzymes. The molasses not only feeds microorganisms but also contains sulfur, which virtually neutralizes the fish smell. Sea Source is a very similar product.

Chelated nutrients. These are used when a direct dose of a particular nutrient is needed to solve a deficiency quickly. Chelated products are chemical structures which encircle and tightly hold micronutrients such as iron, manganese, zinc, and copper. Compost, humus, natural acids—including humic acid—and microorganisms all have natural chelating properties.

Epsom salts. Also known as magnesium sulfate, Epsom salts can be used as a source of magnesium and sulfur. Mixed at 1 tablespoon per gallon of water, it makes an excellent foliar spray to encourage green foliage and flower production. Rosarians have used Epsom salts on roses for more blooms for years.

Garlic/pepper tea. This insect and disease repellent also provides trace minerals. Garlic tea is now available commercially, but garlic/pepper tea isn't yet. However, it is easy to make at home by adding the liquid of two garlic bulbs and two hot peppers to a gallon of water. The concentrate should be used in the spray tank at no more than ¼ cup per gallon. It can be mixed with other sprays. Since the pepper can kill small insects, some organic gardeners use garlic only. Started early in the season and used regularly, garlic spray helps plants repel insect pests and diseases.

Medina. Medina Soil Conditioner is another liquid biostimulant. It stimulates native soil microorganisms and natural biological processes in the soil and in plants. It's also an excellent product for soil detoxification. Medina Plus contains trace elements as well as seaweed. Hastagrow is another seaweed product that contains a low-salt chemical fertilizer.

Molasses. Blackstrap molasses, a product of the cane industry, is very high in natural minerals, enzymes, and amino acids. Combining pure feed-grade blackstrap molasses with any liquid and applying it to crops will increase sugar levels, thus improving plant resistance to chewing and sucking insects. Molasses is an excellent food source to energize the biological life in the soil. *Rates of application:* for soil application, 2–4 quarts per acre; for foliar application, 1 pint per acre on broadleaf plants (such as soybeans, alfalfa, and ornamental plants) and 1 quart per acre on all other crops (such as rice, corn, milo, wheat, and grass).

Hydrogen peroxide. This is water with an extra oxygen molecule (H_2O_2). Not only does it help to heal cuts and scrapes, it is also an excellent addition to most organic spray programs. Its oxidizing effect helps the soil and encourages the beneficial microorganisms on the foliage. It should be used at 8 ounces of 3 percent solution per gallon of water or ½ ounce (1 tablespoon) of 35 percent concentrate per gallon of water.

Humates. These can also be used in foliar sprays. They vary greatly in percentage of humic acid but are an excellent source of carbon and many trace minerals. They can be mixed with any of the above-mentioned products.

Vinegar. Natural vinegars such as apple cider vinegar are

very acidic and loaded with lots of carbon and trace minerals. Use 1 tablespoon per gallon of water.

Vinegar: The Not-So-New Organic Tool

Vinegar is a wonderful organic tool that was discovered by accident ten thousand years ago when wine was accidentally allowed to ferment too long and turned sour. It can be made from many products, including beer, apples, berries, beets, corn, fruits, grains, honey, malt, maple syrup, melons, molasses, potatoes, rice, sorghum, and other foods containing sugar. Natural sugars from these food products are fermented into alcohol, which is then fermented into vinegar.

Fruit vinegar is made from the fermentation of a variety of fruits. Apples are most commonly used, but grapes, peaches, berries, and other fruits also work. The product label will identify the starting ingredients, such as "apple cider vinegar" or "wine vinegar." Malt vinegar is made from the fermentation of barley malt or other cereal grains. Sugar vinegar is made from sugar, syrup, or molasses. White, spirit, or distilled vinegar is made by fermenting distilled alcohol. Distilled white vinegar is made from 190-proof alcohol that is fermented by adding sugar and living bacteria. Natural vinegar contains at least fifty trace minerals.

The strongest vinegar available for general use is 20 percent or 200-grain, meaning that about 20 percent of the liquid is acetic acid. At this strength, which is corrosive enough to eat metal and must be handled carefully in plastic containers, it will obviously kill weeds, making it an effective nonselective organic herbicide. It works best when sprayed full strength during the heat of the day and in full sunlight. While 200-grain (20 percent) material is the best strength for killing weeds, 100-grain (10 percent), which is made by doubling the amount of water in the 200-grain vinegar, seems to work just about as well if used consistently. Moreover, since this diluting process cuts the cost in half, it's usually advisable to go ahead and use the weaker solution.

The other horticultural use for vinegar is in the watering can.

If your water is alkaline, add 1 tablespoon of 50-grain (5 percent) natural apple cider vinegar to each gallon of water to improve the quality of the water for potted plants and bedding. This doesn't have to be done with every watering, though it wouldn't hurt. This technique is especially helpful when trying to grow acid-loving plants such as gardenias, azaleas, and dogwoods. A table-spoon of vinegar per gallon added to the sprayer when foliar-feeding lawns, shrubs, flowers, and trees is also highly beneficial, especially where soil or water is alkaline.

Many of the uses of vinegar date back thousands of years; they include such general applications as antibiotics for wounds, treatment of rashes and bites, prevention of scurvy, pickling and preserving, household cleaning, flavoring, and cooking. Here's a smattering of other uses for vinegar:

Cleaning counter tops. Soak a cloth in white vinegar (5 percent strength) and wipe the surface. This will also help deter ants and other insect pests.

Cleaning garbage disposal. Mix 1 cup of vinegar in enough water to fill an ice tray, and freeze. Run the frozen cubes through the disposal unit and then flush with cold water.

Cleaning shower curtains. Wash plastic shower curtains in the washing machine with one bath towel. Add a cup of white vinegar to the rinse cycle. Tumble-dry briefly. If you don't have time to wash the curtain, just wipe it clean with a cloth or sponge soaked in vinegar.

Removing grease. Clean grease and dirt from exhaust-fan grills and air-conditioner blades and grills with a sponge dipped in undiluted vinegar (5 percent). This also works for grease on the stove and refrigerator.

Keeping cut flowers fresh. Add 1 tablespoon of vinegar and 1 tablespoon of sugar to each quart of warm water to keep cut flowers lasting longer.

Killing fleas and ticks. A teaspoon of vinegar in each gallon of drinking water helps keep your pet free of fleas and ticks.

Unplugging sink drains. Pour a handful of baking soda down the blocked drain and add a cup of vinegar.

Cutting through rust. To free a rusted or corroded bolt, soak it in vinegar.

Removing paint spots. Hot vinegar will remove paint spots from glass.

Ensuring fluffy rice. One teaspoon of vinegar added to water for cooking rice makes it white and fluffy, no matter what type of water is used.

Freshening vegetables. Slightly wilted vegetables can be freshened by soaking them in cold water and vinegar.

As a summer drink. One tablespoon of strawberry or orange vinegar mixed in a glass with 8 ounces of club soda and ice makes a refreshing cold drink.

As a skin treatment. To restore moisture in dry hands, rub them with vinegar.

Among its many other uses, vinegar can also soften hard paintbrushes, stop the sting of both insect bites and sunburn, help prevent sunburned skin from peeling, remove odors and fruit stains, and tenderize tough meat. And you thought vinegar was just for making salad dressing and pickling cucumbers.

For additional information on vinegar and its uses, contact the Vinegar Institute, Suite 500-D, 5775 Peachtree-Dunwoody Road, Atlanta, Georgia 30342, (404) 252-3663.

N-P-K Not Important in Organic Program

Fertilizing with typical high-nitrogen, artificial, water-soluble products doesn't work. Feeding your plants nothing but nitrogen, phosphorus, and potassium (N-P-K)—which is largely what these products contain—is like feeding your kids nothing but white bread. All living organisms need a balance of nutrients. University extension offices continue to emphasize these three nutrients in their fertilizer recommendations; in particular, they emphasize high levels of nitrogen. A 3-1-2 ratio such as 15-5-10 is a common recommendation. There's a debate that's been going on for some time about changing the standard recommendation to a 1-0-0 analysis. We'll see how that turns out.

In any case, the recommendation still contains too much nitrogen, and too much nitrogen can result in several problems. As much as 50 percent of all synthetic nitrogen applied to the soil will leach out, and the half that does reach the plant may be hurting it. Other studies show that a chemical fertilizer containing an excessive amount of nitrogen disrupts the activity and balance of the microflora and microfauna in the soil. A pound of healthy soil contains almost one billion of these living organisms, many of which, such as bacteria, algae, and fungi, are beneficial. Harsh fertilizers also repel larger organisms, such as earthworms.

Severe thatch buildup in lawns is a direct result of the use of high-nitrogen fertilizers. As a result, mechanical thatch-removal programs are often recommended for artificially maintained lawns. Thatch is not a problem in organic programs because earthworms and microbes feed on the grass clippings and other residue and turn them into fertilizer.

The law in most states requires the percentage of nitrogen, phosphorus, and potassium to be listed on fertilizer bags. The numbers on lawn fertilizer bags will range from 28-0-0 to 16-4-8 to 20-10-10. Such amounts of N-P-K are unnecessary. When healthy, the soil will actually produce and release nutrients during the decomposition process, and the microbiotic activity helps release nutrients that are tied up in the soil, as well as the many nutritious trace elements, such as iron, zinc, boron, calcium, chlorine, copper, magnesium, molybdenum, and sulfur, which are also important to a well-balanced soil. Earthworm castings, which provide one of the best of all organic fertilizers, have an N-P-K ratio of less than 1-1-1. It's balance we're looking for, not a glut of fast-acting nutrients.

An overlooked element which is probably more important than all other elements is oxygen. Adding oxygen to most soils can result in much the same effect as using high-nitrogen fertilizer, in that it provokes a healthy response from all plants and gives rise to an immediate green-up. Oxygen can be added to the soil by mechanical means such as aeration or tilling or through the use of many of the organic fertilizers and soil conditioners.

Healthy plants with their extensive root systems can, in fact, be very beneficial for the introduction of oxygen into the all-important top 12 inches of soil. Besides oxygen, the most important ingredient in an organic program is organic matter. Organic matter provides humus, which turns into humic acid—the active ingredient of organic matter. Organic fertilizers that are high in both humus and humic acid are the most highly recommended because the humic acid is immediately available to the plant and causes greening in much the same manner as high-nitrogen fertilizers do. Their use also eliminates one of the objections to the organic program, which is that it takes much longer to get results; this is not the case when using organic fertilizers with high levels of humic acid.

The major causes of plant problems, especially in clay soils, are a lack of oxygen and a lack of organic matter. Poor drainage can add to this problematic situation by depriving the root system of oxygen. Plants can be helped to grow in heavy soils by using an underground drainage system made of a ditch full of gravel or perforated PVC pipe surrounded by gravel (or any physical channel that can take water away from planting areas to a lower spot).

A healthy, living soil doesn't need high levels of N-P-K because nature produces its own nutrients as the microorganisms break down the organic material. Balance is the basis of healthy gardening, and allowing nature to work is simply a matter of patience.

Nitrogen Source—Does The Plant Care?

One of the most frequent arguments against organics concerns the issue of organic versus artificial nitrogen. Organiphobes argue that a plant can't tell the difference between natural and synthetic sources of nitrogen and doesn't care where the nitrogen comes from. They maintain that whether the source is natural or synthetic, nitrogen is in its basic elemental form when it is absorbed by the plant. But they are wrong! It's true that many nutrients are absorbed in their elemental forms, but there is a fatal flaw in this reasoning. There is now sufficient evidence that plants can actually absorb chunks of material or large molecules that break down once they are in the plant. Besides, when organic fertilizers release nitrogen, what's left behind is organic matter and other nutrients, whereas when artificial fertilizers release nitrogen, they leave behind salts and (usually unidentified) fillers. In addition, the harsh levels of nutrients and salts contained in artificial fertilizers are quite detrimental to the living microorganisms which are so critical to healthy, balanced soil.

Besides all that, artificial fertilizers—those that are high in nitrogen and quickly water soluble—bypass many of the natural systems in the soil and glut plants with too much nitrogen. Soil microorganisms, whose major function it is to help fix nitrogen from the air and release it from organic matter, are eliminated from the process. If they aren't needed, they kick their feet up, relax, and shut down. In other words, artificial fertilizers feed the plants but do nothing helpful to the soil—in fact, the high-nitrogen fertilizers can do a considerable amount of harm to the soil, especially over the long term.

Nitrogen is an important nutrient that is necessary for healthy plant growth, but it is not necessary in large quantities or from artificial sources. That should seem obvious to anyone who has ever seen a forest. The use of high-nitrogen, water-soluble, salt-based fertilizers is actually a new addition to agriculture and horticulture. Before the war years, mineral salt fertilizers weren't used to promote plant growth. The world's food supply and landscape gardens were fertilized by low-nitrogen natural materials such as manures, meals, and compost.

Using large quantities of high-nitrogen fertilizers creates many problems. The excessive use of these fertilizers causes an accumulation of nitrates in the soil and groundwater. Nitrates convert into nitrites, the raw materials for chemicals known as nitrosamines, which can cause cancer in animals. That's a pretty good reason to reduce nitrogen inputs right there. Excessive use of high-nitrogen fertilizers also contributes to other serious environmental problems, such as deterioration of soil tilth, the destruction of balanced soil microbiology, the alteration of plant vitamins, proteins, and sugars, increased vulnerability to insects and diseases, and the restriction of natural soil and plant systems.

On the other hand, organic fertilizers feed the soil in a gentle, natural way, and help to stimulate the biological processes that feed the plants by using natural systems which functioned long before we started messing them up. With organic plant foods, *all* the nutrients—not just N-P-K, as supplied by artificial fertilizers—are available to plants when the temperature and moisture are correct.

Yes, nitrogen is nitrogen no matter where it comes from, but there's more to the puzzle. Nothing else good comes along with artificially processed nitrogen. A lot of other nutrients, vitamins, enzymes, acids, and humic material come along with organic sources. It's all a matter of balance: organic fertilizers are usually balanced; artificial ones usually are not.

Differences in Organic Fertilizers

I am delighted that so many new organic products are coming on the market. Fertilizers top the list of new arrivals and, as is to be expected, confusion abounds about which is the best to buy. In general, most of the 100 percent organic fertilizers are effective and are recommended for certain uses. I'll give some general guidelines and then review the specific products I have used.

First of all, watch out for the term "organic-based." There's nothing wrong with these products, unless you want to go organic. They aren't organic. Some are mostly synthetic fertilizers with a little organic matter added. Others are mostly organic with a little urea or other chemical fertilizer added; these are better. Also watch out for the coverage trick: some organic fertilizers come with instructions to apply them to a larger area than they will effectively cover. If you are a beginning organic gardener, the rate to use for all products listed below is 20 pounds per 1,000 square feet, unless otherwise noted. This rate is necessary to start the reversal of the soil's chemical dependency and to begin rebuilding the soil humus. After the soil's health has been improved, applications can be reduced to 10 pounds per 1,000 square feet. Recommended rates of less than this are questionable.

I've written often about the benefits of organic fertilizers, but so far have failed to emphasize one particular issue sufficiently. In a bag of synthetic fertilizer with a 15-5-10 analysis for example, 30 percent of the contents of the bag is fertilizer, while the other 70 percent usually consists of fillers and salts. The N-P-K analysis of an organic fertilizer will be smaller—perhaps 6-2-2, 4-2-0, or 5-2-4—but 100 percent of the ingredients in the bag consist of food for the soil. Organic fertilizers, because they are primarily plant derivatives, contain at least some quantity of all the trace minerals the soil and the plants need, and they often contain at least fifty to sixty trace minerals. Many organic fertilizers contain all ninety-two elements. Organic foods contain carbon, organic matter, humus (which is decomposed organic matter), hormones, enzymes, and beneficial fungi and bacteria.

Organic fertilizers are naturally time-released so they don't glut the plants with nutrients at the wrong time but instead break down and release nutrients when the plants are growing the fastest and need the nutrition most. Most synthetic fertilizers, with the exception of sulfur and plastic-coated products, are water soluble and are immediately available at application.

Here's a rundown of the most available and useful natural organic fertilizers:

Alfalfa meal. Meal made from ground-up alfalfa hay is a terrific organic fertilizer that stimulates microbes very quickly and suppresses many soil-borne diseases. Helpful ingredients include vitamin A, folic acid, nitrogen, potassium, calcium, magnesium, enzymes, amino acids, and trace elements. Its analysis will vary with the crop but will usually be in the 3-1-2 to 5-1-2 range. If possible, buy meal made from alfalfa that has been grown organically. Use at 10–25 pounds per 1,000 square feet.

Bat guano. Yes, this is bat poop from the caves where they live. Bat guano has natural fungicidal qualities and little chance of being contaminated with pesticides or chemicals. It is an excellent supplemental fertilizer for flowers and is best applied once or twice during the growing season. It is very light and dusty, but potent, so don't overuse, and avoid breathing the dust. The analysis will vary with the age of the guano, the nitrogen content diminishing with age, but it is usually around 10-3-1. Use at 10–20 pounds per 1,000 square feet.

Blood meal. When cows are slaughtered, the blood is dried and made into meal. It's expensive but good to use occasionally, although it's also stinky and difficult to apply with a spreader. The analysis can range from 12-2-1 to 11-0-0. Use at 10–20 pounds per 1,000 square feet.

Bone meal. An excellent source of calcium and phosphorus recommended for bulbs, tomatoes, and other vegetables. The analysis will range from 1-12-0 to 4-12-0 with 2–5 percent calcium. Use at 10–20 pounds per 1,000 square feet.

Colloidal phosphate. Also called soft rock phosphate, this is a mixture of fine particles of phosphate suspended in a fine clay base. It is an economic form of natural phosphorus, calcium, and trace minerals. Whereas synthetic phosphate is soluble in water and works too fast, rock phosphate is insoluble in water, will not leach away, and therefore is long lasting. Soft rock phosphate works faster but in a natural way. It has 18 percent phosphorus, 15 percent calcium, and a natural blend of many trace elements. Florida is the primary source. Analysis is usually around 0-20-0. Use at 20–40 pounds per 1,000 square feet.

Compost. As nature's fertilizer, compost should be the key input in any organic program. It is high in organic matter, humus, rock, minerals, humic and other natural acids, and microorganisms. Compost has almost magical healing and growth powers and should be used on any and all soils and on all plants. It can be homemade or purchased commercially. The best composts are those made from a variety of raw organic materials, such as noncontaminated paper, hay, cotton burs, sawdust, paunch manure (cow-intestine contents), leaves, twigs, bark, wood chips, alfalfa, molasses, dead plants, nongreasy food scraps, pecan hulls, grass clippings, and animal manure (the best manure to use being whatever is locally available: chicken, turkey, pig, cattle, horse, rabbit, etc.). The ideal proportions are 75–80 percent vegetative material and 20–25 percent animal manure. The analysis of compost will vary depending on its ingredients but will usually be around 1-1-1. Apply a layer from 1 to 8 inches thick, depending on your budget and the condition of the soil.

Cottonseed meal. One of the best natural fertilizers, cottonseed meal contains a good balance of trace elements and has an acid pH. It has some odor when first applied but is an excellent organic source of nitrogen. The only negative factor is that most cotton is grown on a heavy-duty chemical diet and as a result there is some pesticide residue in the meal. Fortunately for us all, however, the arsenical defoliants have been banned, so there is at least some movement in the right direction. The analysis will vary from 6-2-1 to 7-2-2. Use at 10–20 pounds per 1,000 square feet on turf and in beds and add to compost piles to stimulate microbial activity.

Earthworm castings. Maybe the best all-around organic fertilizer, earthworm castings are high in bacteria, calcium, iron, magnesium, and sulfur and have over sixty identified trace minerals. Encouraging your own earthworm population is the cheapest and best way to get this material. Besides adding nutrients to the soil, earthworms help to aerate it and bring minerals from deep in the ground to the top few inches of soil. N-P-K analysis is less than 1-1-1. Use at 20–40 pounds per 1,000 square feet.

Fish meal. This smelly but powerful natural fertilizer was originally used in this country by Indians for growing corn. Its N-P-K analysis of 8-12-0 makes it pretty hot for an organic fertilizer. Use at 10–20 pounds per 1,000 square feet. Fish meal is a good choice for pushing flower production on annuals and perennials.

Greensand. Also called glauconite, this naturally deposited sedimentary marine material is composed primarily of iron, potassium, aluminum, and magnesium. It is an excellent organic soil amendment with a normal analysis of about 0-1-5. It should be used with other fertilizers to provide a blend of many minerals. Use at 10–20 pounds per 1,000 square feet.

Kelp meal. A natural fertilizer meal made from seaweed, kelp meal has lots of trace minerals. It is an excellent source of plant hormones, which stimulate root growth and regulate plant growth. Seaweed also provides soil-conditioning substances which improve the crumb structure or soil tilth, and is good for stimulating microbes in compost piles. It has an approximate analysis of 1-1-8. Use at 10–20 pounds per 1,000 square feet.

Lava sand. This has been hauled away as a waste product in the past, but it is excellent both as a high-energy soil amendment (although it has an analysis of less than 1-1-1) and as a source of many trace minerals. Use it in seed-germinating trays, pots, landscape beds, and gardens. It is highly recommended for use around sick trees. Use with compost and other organic fertilizers, at 20–40 pounds per 1,000 square feet.

Many manufactured fertilizers are now available that contain 100 percent organic ingredients. They include, but are not limited to, Earthsafe, Garden-Ville Soil Food, GreenSense, GroUp, Harmony, Maestro Gro, Natural Guard, Nitron, Organigro, Ringer, and Sustane. Their analysis varies, and those with the most soluble nitrogen will work fastest, but all 100 percent organic products work, and the choice should be based on ease of application, consistency, and price. Using different products from time to time is a good way to insure a balance of nutrients. Try them all—and let me know which ones work best for you.

Fall Fertilization

To feed or not to feed in the fall? I recommend that gardeners fertilize in the fall, especially if they are still in the soil-building transition from a chemical program. Seasoned organic gardeners can fertilize by simply adding more mulch to the beds and gardens each year. This works if the soil beneath the mulch is healthy and balanced. If the soil is soft, sweet smelling, well aggregated, and full of earthworms, it's probably in pretty good shape. For beginning organic gardeners, it's a good bet that you don't yet have healthy soil. If that's the case, fall is the ideal time to start the program, given that this is when nature applies organic matter to the soil through the defoliation of trees and shrubs. Organic matter in the form of fallen leaves breaks down slowly and turns into rich humus over the winter so that it's ready to help plant growth in the spring. When you apply organic fertilizers, you imitate nature's techniques, but composted materials speed up the process. Fertilizing in the fall will stimulate root growth and improve the soil throughout the winter. When spring comes, plants will have ample fertility for healthy growth. To best imitate nature, wait until after the first hard freeze, but that's not critical. Organic fertilizer can be applied any month of the year, because it's the soil that's being fed, not the plants.

If you decide to fertilize in the fall, use a 100 percent natural organic fertilizer at 20 pounds per 1,000 square feet. These products can be applied with conventional fertilizer spreaders. Natural meals such as cottonseed meal, alfalfa meal, fish meal, blood meal, kelp meal, and soybean meal can also be used. Manure products like cricket waste, bat guano, rabbit manure, and earthworm castings are all excellent fall fertilizer choices. The meals and manure products are not usually pelletized or granulated and therefore aren't easily distributed by a conventional spreader. Some work better than others. I generally apply these materials by hand and use them primarily in smaller areas.

Compost is the best of all organic fall fertilizers. After all, it's nature's own. The only disadvantage of using compost as a fertilizer is that it won't go through a spreader easily and is therefore more trouble and more expensive than the other alternatives. However, if you have the time and the budget, it's the best way to improve lousy bed soil or weedy lawn areas, especially if applied after opening holes in the ground by mechanical aeration. For best results, stab holes in the ground with a turning fork or hand aerator, dump piles of compost on the ground, and rake the material around with a hand garden rake, concrete rake, or, for large areas, a drag made from a piece of chain-link fence.

Greensand, lava sand, and colloidal phosphate are also excellent fall treatments to use if the budget allows. Greensand is a good natural potash source, while colloidal phosphate and lava sand are good natural sources of phosphorus and potash, and all three are loaded with trace minerals. Avoid using a lot of colloidal phosphate (soft rock phosphate) on high-calcium soils, since it contains a lot of calcium. If you have too much calcium already, you don't need more.

The final fall fertilization step for all levels of organic gardeners is a thick application of mulch to all bare soil. Coarse-textured, shredded hardwood bark or shredded native tree chips make the best mulch material for ornamental beds, and alfalfa hay is the best for vegetable gardens and roses. Other good mulches include partially finished compost, pine needles, pecan shells, and cocoa bean shells. Grass areas can be mulched with a light application of compost, but a similar effect can be obtained by raising the cutting height of the mower one more notch. Tall grass and its thatch function as a mulch for turf. Tree leaves can be left on the grass if they are ground up with a mower or grinder. Mulching leaves for bed areas is optional. They can be left as they fall in the beds if you like the appearance of leaves all over the place; it's actually the most natural look you can have, and no, it doesn't cause diseases—if it did, all the forests would be dead!

Mulching will help to protect plants against freeze damage. For additional protection, spray plants sensitive to freeze damage weekly or biweekly with liquid seaweed until the first hard frost. Kelp can provide as much as four degrees of frost protection. Make light spray applications, usually around 1 tablespoon per gallon of water, and spray late in the afternoon for best results.

Fall is a great time to install new plants, especially trees, shrubs, and hardy perennials. These plants will establish root systems during the fall and winter and be ready to take off in the spring. In addition, if you have a vegetable garden area that needs improvement, consider planting a green manure crop of hairy vetch, elbon rye, oats, arrowleaf clover, alfalfa, or Austrian winter peas. Use any combination or all of the above. Till the plants into the soil at least three weeks before planting in the spring. A 50-50 mix of hairy vetch and oats is a popular choice. Hairy vetch has been shown to increase food crop production if mowed in the spring and left to regrow under tomatoes and other transplants.

4 Pest Control

Most Bugs Are Beneficial

Getting rid of all the bugs in your garden is impossible. Even if it were possible, it would be a bad idea. Insects and other invertebrates are an extremely important aspect of organics. Without a basic understanding of the critter world, an organic gardener is at a great disadvantage. Of the millions and millions of insect species, only about 800,000 have been identified and described. It's a surprise to many people to find out that almost all bugs are beneficial. It could be argued that all insects are beneficial if they are in their proper place.

Insects do a great job of controlling themselves if we don't foul up the balance by spraying pesticides. Even the insects we would usually classify as harmful are helpful in their own way. Aphids, for example, are actually an important tool in ensuring the survival of the fittest. They attack plants that are under stress as a result of cultural problems, such as poor drainage, compacted soil, or poor plant selection, and by doing so, they help to eliminate unfit plants. Insects and other pest manifestations are thus only symptoms of more serious problems.

The so-called bad bugs, which account for only 1–2 percent of the insect population, include aphids, ants, bagworms, beetles, borers, caterpillars, crickets, chiggers, chinch bugs, fleas, grasshoppers, grubworms, lacebugs, leafhoppers, leaf miners, mealybugs, mosquitoes, nematodes, pill bugs, spider mites, roaches, scale, squash bugs, slugs, thrips, and whiteflies. Heavy infestations of these allegedly harmful critters can be controlled with organic techniques and products that are much safer than synthetic chemical poisons. Aphids, red spider mites, and other small pests can be controlled with soap and water, while the tougher bugs, such as beetles, can be controlled with pyrethrum, rotenone, sabadilla dust, and horticultural oil. However, spray only when a serious problem exists, because any spray, organic or chemical, will kill more beneficial insects than pests. Soap (nonphosphate and biodegradable) mixed with water at 1 teaspoon per gallon, is the mildest insecticide, but even it will kill some small beneficials. Garlic spray, which is even milder, doesn't kill insects but rather acts as a repellent; when hot pepper juice is added to the garlic, it does become a mild insecticide.

Remember that chemical pesticides can't tell the good guys from the bad guys. The good insects that comprise the vast majority of the population should be protected and, when needed, added to the landscape. They include ladybugs, green lacewings, ground beetles, praying mantids, minute pirate bugs, dragonflies, damselflies, fireflies, assassin bugs, spiders, wasps, and predatory mites. Other forms of helpful wildlife that provide important functions in the balance of nature and should also be protected and encouraged include lizards, frogs, toads, turtles, nonpoisonous snakes, and birds.

My friend Malcolm Beck, the organic expert in San Antonio, once told me about his learning experience with insects. Thirty years ago he had a new vegetable farm and in an attempt to stay up on all the latest techniques was reading an article in an agriculture magazine about the Colorado potato beetle invading farm crops. He looked at his potato plants, and sure enough there were bugs all over the place. He quickly loaded up his sprayer with poison and blasted the critters. A friend advised him too late that unfortunately the bugs were not potato beetles but ladybugs. With the ladybugs gone, the aphids invaded and began to devour his plants, so he had to load up the sprayer again to kill the damaging bugs. The vicious cycle had started. Malcolm was lucky—and also very smart—because this early experience showed him that disturbing the balance of nature is a big mistake. At this point he became a 100 percent organic farmer and proved to himself and to many others that the secret is to work with nature, not to try to control it.

Here's some more information on the good bugs to help you become familiar with and use these friends. In fact, the first attempt at insect pest control should be with the release of beneficial insects.

Spring is the key time to release beneficial insects, since soft, succulent new growth on plants attracts aphids and other critters, especially if you are still using high-nitrogen fertilizers and encouraging unhealthy fast growth. Releasing beneficial insects on a regular schedule and fertilizing with soil-improving materials will provide excellent long-term control. The best bugs to buy and release now are ladybugs, green lacewings, and trichogramma wasps. For a simpler program, stick with ladybugs and green lacewings. Keep them cool and watered, and don't spray anything that will kill them, including organic insecticides. Their favorite food is juicy bad bugs. If you don't have bad bugs, of course, there's no reason to buy and release good bugs.

Aphids are the most common insect pest during the cool spring weather. They can be controlled by ladybugs, which can be purchased in mesh bags or in small box containers that hold about 1,500 bugs to a pint and up to 70,000 bugs in a gallon container. The best way to release ladybugs for the control of aphids is to sprinkle the foliage with water and release the bugs directly on the infested plants at about dusk.

Green lacewings are even more beneficial because they control so many different kinds of pests. Containers of eggs or larvae mixed in sawdust can be purchased for release to control aphids, spider mites, thrips, caterpillars, and other pests. Again, it's best to release them during the cooler part of the day. These insects are very small, but aggressive and voracious. The adult is about ½-inch long and feeds on honeydew and nectar. The ferocious larvae actually do the insect control. It's a good idea to do a series of releases of green lacewings throughout the spring and summer until natural populations are established.

Trichogramma wasps should be released from small containers or cards attached to plants that are having problems with pecan nut casebearers, cabbage worms, tomato hornworms, corn earworms, or many orchard pests. These beneficial insects are very tiny, gnatlike parasitic wasps. Again, a series of releases is desirable.

Here, in more detail, are descriptions of some of the most beneficial insects and other critters:

Ladybug (*Hippodamia convergens*). The ladybug, or ladybird beetle, is a great friend. Ladybugs are the most popular and most universally known of all the beneficial insects. There are several hundred species in North America, and all are beneficial. The most common native varieties are orange with black spots, gray with black spots, and black with two red spots. The black and gray varieties are arboreal and therefore usually seen in trees. The native variety, *Hippodamia convergens*, orange with black spots, is the most readily available commercially. All ladybugs should be protected.

After buying your package of ladybugs, leave the bag or carton sealed and place in the refrigerator if the temperature is above 90° F. Waiting until evening to release them helps limit their tendency to fly off back to California. To release ladybugs, open the container and scatter them on plants after watering the foliage. If the bugs start to fly away, put them back in the refrigerator for two days. Ladybugs will store well for several days at 35–45°. Most of them will remain dormant and alive at these cool temperatures, although storage tends to dry them out, and a few will die.

To thrive and reproduce, ladybugs need flowering plants for a source of nectar and pollen. Legumes such as peas, beans, clover, and alfalfa are especially good, but any flowering plant will help. Artificial food can be made by diluting a little honey with a small amount of water and mixing in a little brewer's yeast or bee pollen. Smear small amounts of this mixture on small pieces of waxed paper and fasten them to plants. Replace these every 5–6 days, or when they become moldy. Keep any extra food refrigerated between feedings. This is a temporary, artificial technique, so only use it in the beginning. Aphids are the ladybug's favorite real food.

When using ladybugs indoors or in a greenhouse, screen off any openings to prevent their escape.

Green lacewing (*Chrysopa carnea*). Green lacewings are the most effective beneficial insect. They are fragile and light green with lustrous yellow eyes. Adults, which are about ½-inch long, feed on honeydew, nectar, and pollen. They aren't really terribly beneficial—they just fly around, look pretty, and mate. Nice life! The green lacewing's larvae are the hard workers. They are voracious eaters of aphids, red spider mites, thrips, mealybugs, cottony cushion scale, and many species of worms.

Lacewing larvae are known as "aphid lions" when they emerge from the eggs, which are very small (a thimble will hold about 10,000 of them) and appear on the end of the white filaments attached to leaves or stems. The gray larvae look like tiny alligators and grow to almost ½ inch in length in 2–3 weeks, after which they pupate by spinning silken threads into small oval cocoons. Adults emerge in about five days by cutting a hole in the cocoon.

To store lacewings prior to release, refrigerate the eggs or larvae for a few days at 38 to 45° F. This will delay development but not hurt the eggs. Do not freeze.

To release green lacewings, hand sprinkle eggs and larvae wherever harmful insects exist or are suspected. Even if put in the wrong place, they will travel 100 feet if necessary for their first meal. A pill bottle with a ¼-inch hole in the cap is a good device for distributing the eggs. A saltshaker will work if the size of the holes is increased. Watch out for ants—they will eat the eggs like jelly beans. Biweekly releases of 2,000 eggs per residential lot or per acre are ideal.

Praying mantids. Praying mantids are friendly to people

but will eat any insect, especially caterpillars, grasshoppers, and beetles, and even their own kind. They are not discriminating; they will eat beneficial insects as well as pests. Be careful not to confuse the egg cases with asps, soft hairy insect larvae with a powerful sting. The native praying mantis egg case looks very similar to an asp, but it is hard, like papier-mâché, while the asp is soft and hairlike. Praying mantids make good pets and pretty good pest-control helpers. They can even be used indoors.

Spiders. Most spiders are not only harmless, but highly beneficial, helping to control many insect pests that attack vegetable and ornamental gardens. The black widow and the brown recluse are the exceptions. You may never see a brown recluse because they are reclusive. They live in dark corners in closets, etc., and move about at night. The female black widow is easy to identify by the red hourglass shape on her abdomen. Beware of her venomous sting—it is very powerful and can cause illness or even death. The much smaller male isn't much trouble; in fact, the female eats him alive after mating. Spiders are a great help in controlling moths whose larvae feed on apples, pecans, and other orchard crops. They also eat aphids on fruit trees and ornamental plants.

Predatory mites. The predatory mite (*Phyoseiulus persimilis*) is orange in the adult stage and pale salmon in its immature stage. It can be differentiated from the pest mite—the "red" two-spotted spider mite—by its lack of spots. Predatory mites have pear-shaped bodies, and their front legs are longer than those of pest mites. Beneficial mites move about quickly when disturbed or exposed to bright light and multiply much faster than pest mites. Females lay about fifty eggs a day, and each mite eats from five to twenty spider mites (or eggs) per day.

Release predatory mites at the first sign of spider-mite damage. Strong blasts of water are effective prior to release. If there is more than an average of one pest mite per leaf, you will probably need to reduce the population with organic sprays such as insecticidal soaps or garlic/pepper tea and seaweed before releasing the predatory mites.

Wasps. Most wasps are beneficial—probably all of them, even the stinging kind. They like all caterpillars, and one of their favorite foods is the tent caterpillar that often disfigures pecan and other shade trees. The tiny trichogramma wasp can be easily purchased and is very effective for controlling cutworms, moths, and the pecan nut casebearer. It lays its eggs on the eggs of the pest. When the wasp's eggs hatch, the larvae feed on the pest's eggs. For best results, trichogramma wasps should be released once every two weeks after bud break in the spring. Use a minimum of 4,000 wasps per ¼ acre at each release.

Trichogramma wasps and most of the smaller wasps don't sting at all. Even the stinging wasps such as yellow jackets will sting only if you threaten them. Mud daubers will sting only if you try to catch them. The mud dauber's favorite food is the black widow spider. Unless a wasp nest is located where a child might bump into it, it should be left in place. If the nest is in a dangerous location, spray the wasps with water and then, while they are on the ground and unable to fly, move the nest to a higher, safer place and reattach it with a nail. The wasps will go right back to it as if nothing had happened. You might get stung, so don't do this if you are highly allergic to wasp stings.

Whitefly parasite (*Encarsia formosa*). Whitefly parasites can help control pests that cause serious damage to tomatoes, cucumbers, and ornamental plants. Smaller than the head of a pin, they are tiny yellow miniature wasps that attack the whitefly in its immature stages, laying eggs in the third and fourth stages, while feeding on the first and second stages. Early, preventative applications of *Encarsia formosa* prior to heavy infestation are recommended. They are expensive, however, and should only be used as part of an overall organic program.

Nematodes. There are various species of nematodes, some of which are harmful to plants, while others are free living and feed on organic debris, microorganisms, and other nematodes. Beneficial nematodes are microscopic roundworms. They can be purchased and used to control cutworms, army worms, corn rootworms, cabbage loopers, Colorado potato beetles, grubs, and other soil pests. Nematodes control insect pests by entering through the mouth or other body openings and, once inside the host, feeding and reproducing until the pest is dead. New nematodes emerge in search of new victims. If pest infestations are present, the ideal schedule consists of early applications prior to heavy infestation, followed by monthly follow-up applications. Once balance is reached, no more releases are necessary.

There are many other highly beneficial insects and other invertebrates, including mites for controlling thrips and fire ants; assassin and wheel bugs, which feed on several of the larger insect pests; and various ground beetles that feed on various harmful insects. Even the children's favorite "lightning bug," or firefly is quite helpful in controlling pests. Firefly larvae like the taste of young slugs.

To provide a proper habitat for beneficial insects, simply go organic. If you stop spraying poisons, limit other toxic materials—even the organic sprays—and allow nature's systems to function, the helpful insects will stay around and help you enjoy your gardens.

There are three ways of purchasing and distributing beneficial insects. The first is to go to the garden shop and buy an "empty box," containing only an order form. You send the order form to the insectary, which then delivers the beneficial insects directly to you. This eliminates delay in shipping and storage and the risk of high temperatures or other environmental changes that might destroy the animals. It takes about ten days to receive the bugs. The second method is to order them directly from the insectaries. The third method is to buy them directly from your local nursery or feed store.

Here's a schedule for insect release. The amounts given are per acre or per residential lot. This is a suggested starting point and should be adjusted to fit each specific site. Your garden or farm may need more or fewer insects. The exact program should be based on the existing populations of insects.

BENEFICIAL INSECT RELEASE SCHEDULE

April–May: Release trichogramma wasps at 10,000 to 20,000 eggs weekly for six weeks.
Release green lacewings at 4,000 eggs weekly for four weeks.
Release ladybugs as needed on aphid infested plants.
May–September: Release green lacewings at 2,000 eggs every two weeks.

SOURCES OF BENEFICIAL BUGS

The best source is your local neighborhood nursery or feed store; failing that, here's a list of suppliers:

Arbico, P.O. Box 4247, Tucson, AZ 85738, 800/827-2847

Biofac, P.O. Box 87, Mathis, TX 78368, 800/233-4914

Bio Insect Control, 710 S. Columbia, Plainview, TX 79072, 806/293-5861

Gardens Alive, 5100 Schenley Place, Lawrencebury, IN 47025, 812/537-8650

Integrated Pest Management, 305 Agostino Road, San Gabriel, CA 91776, 818/287-1101

Kunafin, Rt. 1 Box 39, Quemado, TX 78877, 800/832-1113

M & R Durango, P.O. Box 886, Bayfield, CO 81122, 800/526-4075

Natural Gardening Research, P.O. Box 149, Sunman, IN 47041, 812/623-3800

Nature's Control, P.O. Box 35, Medford, OR 97501, 503/899-8318

OrCon, Inc., 5132 Venice Blvd., Los Angeles, CA 90019, 213/937-7444

Organic Pest Management, P.O. Box 55267, Seattle, WA 98155, 206/367-7007

Pest Management Services, Rt. 12 Box 346-31, Lubbock, TX 79424, 806/794-6761

Rincon-Vitova Insectaries, P.O. Box 95, Oak View, CA 93022, 800/248-2847

Diatomaceous Earth—Nature's Natural Insecticide

One reason I don't like insecticides of any kind is that most are nonselective, killing both the bad and the good insects. A more important reason is that insecticides are extremely dangerous to pets and children. They are also harmful to adults, especially the sick and the elderly, and to the soil as well.

Some foolish people continue to say that chemical insecticides can be safely used even on vegetables and fruits if the label directions are followed closely. I don't believe that! Even at the recommended rates, synthetic chemical pesticides don't occur naturally, and we aren't sure what long-term effect these complex chemicals have, so why should we be comfortable using them? What I would recommend instead is this: rather than using synthetic poisons, use organic products. Organic pesticides are usually made from naturally occurring materials, such as the plant derivatives pyrethrum, rotenone, and sabadilla. One of my favorite insect-control products comes from the earth—it's called diatomaceous earth.

WHAT IS DIATOMACEOUS EARTH?

Diatomaceous earth (D.E. for short) consists of the remains of microscopic one-celled plants (phytoplankton) called diatoms that lived in the oceans that once covered the western part of the United States and other parts of the world. The huge deposits that were left behind when the water receded are now mined and have several important uses—for example, in toothpaste and in filtering devices for beer and swimming pools. D.E. also makes a very effective insecticide.

The insecticidal quality of D.E. is a result of the razor-sharp edges of the diatom remains. When insects come in contact with it, the sharp edges lacerate their waxy exoskeletons and then the powdery D.E. absorbs their body fluids, causing them to die from dehydration.

There is no residual danger. In fact, D.E. is actually beneficial to the soil, since it's loaded with trace minerals—it's made up of approximately 3 percent magnesium, 86 percent silicon, 5 percent sodium, and 2 percent iron, and has many other trace minerals, such as titanium, boron, manganese, copper, and zirconium. However, there are a few facts about D.E. that you should be aware of.

D.E. is very dusty and can cause lung problems if breathed heavily, so always wear a good dust mask when applying it dry, or stand upwind.

D.E. sold for swimming-pool filters is ineffective for insect control because it has been heated and chemically treated. The sharp edges have been removed.

D.E. will kill beneficial insects too, so use it sparingly to kill problem infestations of harmful insects only, and don't use too often.

D.E. can be applied in a variety of ways. To use it for flea and tick control, apply a light dusting over the lawn, in dog runs, and around pets' bedding or favorite resting spots, and sprinkle a little on your pet between baths of a mild solution of biodegradable nonphosphate soap (such as Neo-Life, Shaklee's, or one of the herbal soaps made for pets) and water at 1 teaspoon per gallon. Avoid dips and soaps containing chemical insecticides.

One of the best uses of D.E. is to add it to pet or livestock food. Used at 1 percent of the food volume, it controls internal parasites, improves digestion, and provides valuable trace minerals.

The best way to apply the dust over a large area is with a lightweight apparatus called a Dustin' Mizer, or with some other similar blower. It can be applied by hand, but this wastes material and will dry your skin. To apply it with water, mix ¼ cup of D.E. in a gallon of water and apply to the lawn and/or shrubs where the problem exists.

Here are some of the common questions I get on diatomaceous earth:

Is D.E. dangerous to my pets, me, or my family? Since D.E. is dusty and abrasive, it can cause lung damage if breathed heavily. Remember that breathing any dusty material can be dangerous. Be sure to wear a dust mask if applying D.E. with a dry blower. Mixing it into a water spray eliminates most of these problems. D.E. will not hurt earthworms or beneficial soil microorganisms. While it is one of the few pesticides in the world classified as non-toxic, I'm not entirely comfortable with that—anything can be toxic if overused or misused.

How much diatomaceous earth should I feed my animals? The feeding rations suggested by suppliers and users include:

1 percent by weight of D.E. in ground, dry feed
5 percent by weight in grain
5 ounces (1 cup) daily ration for horses
1 tablespoon per day for large dogs (over 55 pounds)
1 teaspoon per day for small dogs, puppies, and cats

Does spraying D.E. in a wet solution work as well as the dry dust? The wet spray method does work, but only after the liquid has dried. Mix between 1 and 4 tablespoons D.E. per gallon of water and spray on the lawn, shrubs, tree trunks, and building foundations. When the mixture dries, it has the same abrasive and dehydrating powers as the dry dust. When sprayed wet, the material covers the foliage and other surfaces better than when dusted dry, thus giving better insect control. It seems to last longer when applied wet, but the dry application is usually more effective at killing insects quickly.

Can I mix D.E. with other sprays? Yes, it can be mixed with other organic products, such as seaweed, fish emulsion, garlic tea, and biostimulators. It would be silly to mix D.E. with chemical insecticides. In fact it's silly to use synthetic toxic pesticides for anything.

Is diatomaceous earth registered by the EPA and labeled for insect control? Yes! Although some people would have you believe that D.E. is untested, unlabeled, and therefore unsafe for use, in fact it has been used for years in the food-processing industry to eliminate weevil and other insect infestations in stored grains. There are currently dozens of registrations of D.E. with the EPA for various insecticidal and food-supplement uses. D.E., with and without pyrethrins and piperonyl butoxide, is registered and labeled for controlling fleas, ants, roaches, and many other pests.

Organic gardeners and farmers have been using the product for years to control slugs, chinch bugs, crickets, and grasshoppers. I recommend diatomaceous earth, but only the raw, natural material, and only if it is used sparingly. It should never be overused, and care should always be taken to avoid breathing this or any other dusty material.

Oil Sprays

There are three types of spray oils: dormant, horticultural, and vegetable.

Dormant oil sprays smother overwintering scale insects, summer-weight horticultural oils kill various bugs, and vegetable oils have many surprising uses—in salad dressing, in bug sprays, on rusty tools, and for lubricating drilling equipment.

As early as 1880, kerosene and crude petroleum formulations were used against scale insects, but because these impure products often injured trees and other plants, their use was controversial. Liquid lime sulfur was used on San Jose scale in the early 1900s until it was discovered that a 2 percent solution of light lubrication oil worked better. Oil sprays became the primary tool at this point because they were much more effective against overwintering insects such as leaf rollers, aphids, spider mites, thrips, and scale.

Then came World War II, and oils took a back seat to the wonder poison—DDT. I still vividly remember running down the street behind the fogging truck. Fortunately, DDT was later banned because of its persistence in the environment—it built up in the food chain and was a major cause of death to bald eagles and other endangered species, and in addition, many insects became resistant to DDT, and it actually increased certain insect problems by killing the natural predators more readily than the targeted pest.

Advances in oil-spray technology occurred in the 1950s, but many in the green industry were still reluctant to use it from fear of phytotoxicity (leaf burn) resulting from impurities in the oil. That problem was later overcome by removing the impurities.

Dormant oils have a lower volatility and more insect-killing power than the other oils, but as a result they can be more toxic to plants. Dormant oils should be used only during the winter months when plants are dormant.

Horticultural oils, also petroleum based, are lighter, less phytotoxic, more volatile, and less effective on insects than dormant oils, but they can be used during the heat of summer on many hard-to-kill bugs. The oil itself is not toxic to plants, but some of the impurities in it are. The purity of horticultural oils is indicated by the UR (unsulfonated residue) rating, which is the quantity of oil that is free of unsaturated hydrocarbons. The cleanest horticultural oils on the market today have UR indexes from 95 percent to as high as 99 percent. Horticultural oils are the lightest and most nearly pure petroleum oils. Like dormant oils, they can be used for spraying pecan and fruit trees, but they are also effective on shrubs and flowers that have scale or other insect infestations. They degrade quickly by evaporation, are not poisonous to the applicator, do not corrode equipment, and kill a wide range of insects.

Vegetable oils are plant extracts. They are environmentally safe, degrade quickly by evaporation, work well in organic programs, are not poisonous to the applicator, do not corrode the spray equipment, and kill a wide range of insects. Homemade vegetable-oil concentrate can be made by mixing 1 cup vegetable oil and 1 tablespoon soap in a gallon of water. Then use 1 cup of concentrate per gallon of spray. Some gardeners use a simpler formula: 1 tablespoon vegetable oil and 1 teaspoon soap in 1 gallon of water. Acceptable oils for this use include canola, soybean, corn, sunflower, cottonseed, and olive.

Oils have some disadvantages. All oils can burn sensitive plants or cause branch dieback if improperly applied or overused. The volatile summer oils are a source of air pollution, and, most important, oils are nonselective. They kill beneficial as well as harmful insects. I canceled the spraying of dormant oil on one large commercial project because the red oaks on the property were covered with clusters of yellow eggs which were to become scale-eating ladybugs.

Here are some oil application guidelines:

Don't spray dormant oil if the temperature is below 40° F. Don't spray summer oil if the temperature is above 100° unless the humidity is low.

Don't spray oil if leaves are wet, rain is expected, or the humidity is high.

Apply the oil according to label rates and don't overapply.

Don't spray dormant oil unless the plants are totally dormant.

Be careful in using oils on sensitive plants, such as azalea, maple, and smoketree. Follow the label recommendations, and don't spray if there's a doubt.

Keep the oil and water mixture well shaken; otherwise the oil will separate quickly, become too concentrated, and damage plants. Continue to shake the mix as you spray.

How do oils kill insects? There are three theories—choose the one you like: (1) Oils suffocate bugs by blocking their breathing spiracles. (2) Oils combine with fatty acids in the insect to create poisons. (3) Oils provide residues which disrupt the feeding habits of sucking insects.

I have mixed feelings about all the oil sprays because of their nonselectivity. Working with nature's systems is always better than upsetting them. Oils should be used only for severe infestations, and even vegetable oil should be used very sparingly. Oils should not be used as preventative sprays. Preventative pesticide spraying grossly violates the organic program and common sense. Once a site's overall biodiversity has been reestablished and a healthy population of beneficial insects exists, pesticides of all kinds, including safe oils, should be avoided.

Oil sprays are sometimes a necessary part of a transition program from chemicals to organics. I hope you spray with oils only as a last resort when serious infestations exist and that next year will find your garden in such a healthy, balanced condition that the oil spray won't be necessary.

Herbs for Landscape and Pest Control

Herbs have a great many more uses than those in the culinary world. For starters, many herbs make excellent landscape plants. The bush-type rosemary, for example, is tough, drought tolerant, and even freeze resistant in the south. Other shrublike herbs include myrtle, germander, santolina, and thyme. These make excellent permanent plants, and they are all evergreen in the warmer parts of the country.

Perennial herbs make marvelous additions to the garden, adding fragrance, foliage texture, and flower color. The most beautiful and easiest to grow include artemisia (soft silvery-gray foliage in summer), garlic and onion chives (summer flowers of white and lavender), sweet marigold (yellow flowers late summer into fall), germander (delicate evergreen texture), mealy blue salvia (blue flowers in summer), Gregg salvia (red, pink, or white flowers all summer in the south), yarrow (lovely delicate foliage and yellow, white, pink, or red flowers in summer), purple cone-flower (beautiful white or purple-pink flowers in summer), ginkgo (a beautiful herb tree with gorgeous fall color), and elderberry (a spring-flowering herb with berries in late summer and fall).

Some herbs make excellent groundcovers. Lamb's ear is a soft-textured, light gray-green herb good for small areas; prostrate rosemary is a low-growing version of the regular rosemary; lamium is a silvery-leafed groundcover good for partially shaded areas; pennyroyal is a tough, low-growing evergreen ground-

HERBS FOR COMPANION PLANTING

Herb	Companions	Pests Affected
Basil	Tomatoes; *dislikes rue*	Flies, mosquitoes
Borage	Tomatoes, squash, strawberries	Tomato worms
Calendula	Tomatoes	Tomato worms, asparagus beetle
Camomile	Cabbages	Diamondback moths
Caraway	(Loosens soil)	
Catnip	Lamb's ear	Flea beetles
Chervil	Radishes	Several soil insects
Chives	Carrots	Several soil insects
Dead nettle	Potatoes	Potato bugs
Dill	Cabbages	Cabbage moths
Fennel	*Dislikes most plants*	
Flax	Carrots, potatoes	Several soil insects
Garlic	Roses, raspberries	Aphids, beetles, weevils, borers, spider mites, plum curculio
Henbit	(General insect repellent)	Most insects
Horseradish	(Plant at corners of potato patch)	Potato bugs
Hyssop	Cabbages, grapes	Leaf-cutting insects
Marigolds	Most vegetables	Beetles, nematodes
Mint	Cabbages, tomatoes	White cabbage moths
Nasturtium	Radishes, cabbages, cucurbits	Aphids, squash bugs, whiteflies, striped cucumber beetles
Petunia	Beans	Bean beetles
Rosemary	Cabbages, beans, carrots, sage	Cabbage moths, beetles, mosquitoes, slugs, carrot flies
Rue	Roses, raspberries	Beetles, cats
Sage	Rosemary, cabbages, carrots; *dislikes cucumbers*	Moths, flies, ticks, carrot flies
Southern-wood	Cabbages	Cabbage moths
Summer savory	Beans, onions	Bean beetles
Tansy	Roses, fruit trees	Most flying insects, beetles, squash bugs, ants, borers, cutworms
Thyme	Cabbages	
Wormwood		Moths
Yarrow	(Plant along borders, paths, and near aromatic herbs; enhances production of essential oils)	

cover that is excellent for use between stepping stones; and creeping thyme not only is a durable groundcover but also has flowers in a range of colors from white to lavender. Even Greek oregano makes a good groundcover or low shrub.

The delightful fragrances produced by herbs are common knowledge, but not everyone knows about their insecticidal qualities. The herbs listed in the table may be planted among the other vegetable and ornamental plants in your gardens to help ward off the listed pests.

Traditionally, herbs are defined as herbaceous plants used to flavor foods, make teas, provide medicinal properties, and offer up fragrances. I hope that you will soon learn through personal experience that herbs have many other benefits, not the least of which is that they are easy to grow, look good, smell good, and taste good. Some even make you feel better.

Worst Bugs

MOSQUITOES

About fifty years ago my grandfather appeared before the members of the Pittsburg, Texas, city council and told them that a big insect problem was about to happen. The weather had been unusually wet, and Grandad knew that the mosquitoes would soon take over.

The council didn't listen to his idea about spraying a light coating of oil over the surface of all the ponds and lakes, so he decided to take matters into his own hands. He stopped at several local gas stations and filled pop bottles with used oil. Even though the mosquitoes had already started to emerge from the ponds and attack people, Grandad ended the problem by simply throwing the oil-filled pop bottles into every pond he could find in Camp County. The mosquito problem was eliminated.

Now, I don't recommend that you all run down to the corner gas station and start dumping motor oil in the lakes and streams; we don't need a mini version of the Alaska oil spill—but the lesson is good. The way to control mosquitoes is not to spray poisonous chemicals into the air and onto your skin in an attempt to eliminate the adults. Proper mosquito control is achieved by killing the larvae of the insects in the water where they breed and grow. Horticultural oils are among the cleanest oils to use to lightly coat the surface of standing water. Restraint is the key—don't use too much.

Many cities have a mosquito problem resulting from heavy spring rains every year. As in the California cities that suffered from medfly infestations, the remedy may appear to lie in spraying a chemical poison. That's a bad idea, however, because you don't control mosquitoes by spraying the air with poison chemicals. Chemical insecticides such as Malathion, Dursban, and Diazinon kill not only the target insect pests but also a large percentage of beneficial insects such as fireflies, dragonflies, honeybees, ladybugs, and green lacewings.

The proper way to control mosquitoes is to treat the breeding areas—the ponds, lakes, creeks, trapped water, and other wet places where the eggs are laid, hatch into larvae, and then turn into adults.

Yes, mosquitoes are pests—in fact they are a menace. Not only can they easily spoil a fancy garden party, they can cause malaria, encephalitis, and other serious diseases. Control to prevent the pest from spreading serious diseases is important, but it's also important to note that more home repellents are used in futile attempts to control mosquitoes than for any other home insect pest. The problem with most insecticides is that they don't work. Spraying the air to try to control mosquitoes is not only a waste of time, energy, and money—it is dangerous. It would be better to run around your neighborhood swinging a flyswatter. To really control mosquitoes, you have to treat the breeding water.

Malathion, a chemical pesticide often used to control mosquitoes, is said to be safe for both people and the environment because it breaks down relatively quickly—but relatively quickly compared to what? I have serious doubts about the safety of a product that will damage the paint on cars. As malathion and other chemical insecticides break down, the resulting compounds (metabolites) may actually be more toxic and more dangerous than the original compounds. It's simply a bad idea to use them. There are safer and more effective ways of controlling mosquito outbreaks.

In most years the breeding places can be reduced by providing good drainage, eliminating swampy areas where practical, and dumping the water out of vessels such as pots, old tires, and other containers that hold stagnant water. During wet years, the amount of standing water that accumulates is immense.

Airplanes may be needed for large-scale control, but homeowners can kill mosquitoes in the breeding ponds and puddles by applying organic controls to the water surface. Safe products include garlic tea, instant coffee, mineral oil, and *Bacillus thuringiensis* 'Israelensis' (Bti). Garlic tea can be made by grinding garlic bulbs and pouring the slurry into the standing water. For this purpose, straining the solids out isn't necessary. Instant-coffee crystals can be put into stagnant water at about 2 tablespoons per 100 square feet of water surface. Mineral oil can be used by itself or mixed with one of the other materials to make an effective mosquito control.

The best product for controlling these miserable pests is Bti. *Bacillus thuringiensis* is sold as Dipel or Thuricide for biological control of caterpillars and loopers. The strain 'Israelensis' is specifically targeted at mosquito larvae. It can be bought in granular form or as floating briquettes, which are the longer lasting and easier to use. Use one briquette per 100 square feet of water surface. Bti is sold under the names Bactimos, Teknar, Vectobac, and Mosquito Attack. It is an organic product and will not harm fish or aquatic plants.

Another low-toxicity product, Altosid, is a growth regulator to prevent the adult mosquito from emerging from the larval stage. This product is synthetic but biodegrades quickly and is less harmful to the environment than insecticides. It too is available in briquette form. Use one briquette per 100 square feet.

Deep, flowing water requires a heavier application, but most mosquitoes breed and reproduce in shallow, stagnant water.

Wildlife can help a lot with mosquito control. Night hawks, barn swallows, whippoorwills, bats, purple martins, dragonflies, water fowl, frogs, and fish find mosquitoes a favorite evening treat. Fish such as the tiny and very common gambusia provide terrific mosquito control. The presence of such beneficial wildlife is another important reason I don't like, use, or recommend harsh chemical pesticides that are sprayed in a general application.

To rid your garden of adult flying and biting mosquitoes, try to use something a little safer than the chemical insecticides. Solutions worth trying include citronella candles or lamps, pennyroyal mint crushed and spread around the party area, and tansy and pennyroyal mint planted near doorways and gathering places. Electrocuting lamps are said to kill large numbers of mosquitoes, but the noise of the "cracking-bug-zappers" is more annoying than the mosquitoes—not to mention that the percentage of kill is exaggerated and they also kill beneficial insects.

For the quick fix, if you have a big party with a lot of people who don't eat enough garlic to repel mosquitoes, spray the foliage of trees and shrubs with any D.E./pyrethrum product or a citrus oil spray. These products will kill the adult mosquitoes that rest on the cool underside of leaves during the heat of the day. For added power, use a little nonphosphate soap or mineral oil in the mixture. Not only will this organic method solve an immediate insect problem—your garden won't smell like the inside of a chemical plant. If you are planning to serve Italian food, spray the foliage with garlic tea and mineral oil and put your guests in the proper mood.

No matter which organic method you choose, they are all better than the chemical alternatives.

FLEAS AND TICKS

I get lots of calls and letters about organic flea control. (To be honest, I get lots of calls about how to control fleas in any way—

organic, chemical, nuclear—just get rid of 'em!) I'm delighted that so many people are choosing the alternative route, but not surprised, since the chemical poison route doesn't work as well, and that fact is finally sinking in.

There are no silver bullets for fleas and ticks. No single magic organic or chemical product exists that will completely control these pests and leave your good bugs, pets, and family alive and healthy.

There's only one way to control fleas and ticks successfully: use the holistic approach. That's not an exotic religion—it simply means that the "whole" must be managed. Comprehensive programs work and are not more trouble than applying chemical poisons—quite the contrary. Trouble comes from continuing to spray and poison yourself and your animals and never getting the pest problem under control.

To begin with fleas, it's important to understand their life cycle. The most common flea is called the cat flea. It attacks cats and dogs as well as rats, chickens, opossums, raccoons, squirrels, and other warm-blooded animals. Fleas have four developmental stages: egg, larva, pupa, and adult. Optimum conditions for egg hatching and flea development are 65 to 80° F and 70 percent humidity. Remember those numbers; they are important. When it's 95° next summer and you have fleas, the problem may be in the house—not out in the yard. Fleas like dark, damp, cool spots.

The secret to controlling fleas is to control the eggs and larvae, which are far more numerous than the adults. Adult fleas usually make up only about 2 percent of the total population. It's important to remember that the larvae don't feed on animals as the adults do; instead, they feed on organic debris, primarily dry blood. That's why keeping the pets and the environment clean is so important. Flea larvae live wherever the eggs have fallen, not on the animals, nor do they bite animals or humans. However, they do grow up to be adults and bite people unless you murder them while they're young.

To eliminate flea problems, I recommend the following eight-step program. If you are ready to stop dumping toxic chemicals on your lawn, gardens, carpets, furniture, pets, and yourself, here's my holistic flea program:

1. ***Organic grounds maintenance.*** Allowing biodiversity to reestablish creates competition—lots of different kinds of insects and microbes compete with each other for territory and food. When pesticides are used, that natural balance is destroyed.

2. ***Diet.*** Feed pets a balanced, nutritious diet of your own cooking or an organic pet food. Avoid processed foods that contain chemical preservatives. Ethoxyquin, for example, is a pesticide used as a preservative in many pet foods. BHT and BHA are other chemical preservatives to avoid.

I give my dogs a daily supplement. It used to consist of a little garlic, a little D.E., and a little food-grade kelp, sprinkled on their food—about ⅓ of each, the total volume being 2 percent of the food or less. More recently, I have started using a mixture of D.E. and the Missing Link, a high-quality food supplement for dogs, cats, horses, and even people that contains the essential fatty acids from flax and other grains. I add the supplement daily because the dogs sit and stare at me until I do it. They love the taste, and their coats look great. Another supplement they like a lot is Natural Animal Food Supplement, from the EcoSafe company. It's a blend of D.E., garlic, and a long list of other herbs. Brewer's yeast sprinkled on pet food is some help, but be careful—some animals are allergic to yeast. Garlic and yeast repel fleas and ticks, and D.E. is a natural wormer and aids in digestion, according to the USDA. Buy preservative-free garlic powder and yeast. If the mixing sounds too complicated, just use food-grade D.E. daily. Use about a teaspoon for small dogs and cats and a tablespoon for large dogs. For livestock, about 1–2 percent of the food ratio should be D.E. If you want to cook and have time to, here are two good basic recipes for your pets:

For dogs
50 percent whole grain (rice, barley, etc.)
25 percent meat
25 percent steamed vegetables

For cats
50 percent lean meat
25 percent steamed vegetables
25 percent grain

Despite what you may have heard before, table scraps are good for your pets, assuming you have a decent diet. Varying their diet from time to time helps provide a good blend of vitamins and minerals.

3. Cleaning. Because flea larvae must have organic matter, primarily dry blood, to feed on, vacuum frequently, rake and sweep dog runs and sleeping areas regularly, and pick up and thoroughly compost pet waste. Keeping the pet areas clean helps to starve the fleas out. Remove trash, scrap boards, and other debris that can harbor fleas. It's best to establish a regular sleeping area for your pets and restrict them to areas that can be cleaned easily and often. Carpeted areas are the hardest to keep clean. A weekly vacuuming will remove most fleas, their eggs, and the food which the larvae need for growth.

4. Grooming. Bathe pets weekly or as needed, but only with mild, nontoxic soaps. Herbal shampoos are good, but any low-phosphate, biodegradable soap will work. Shampoos containing citrus oil are also effective. Avoid all soaps containing pesticides. Leave shampoo on pets for five minutes before rinsing. If not done too often, bathing pets helps greatly because soap kills fleas. Brushing regularly is even better because it cleans and stimulates the natural oils in pets' coats. These oils help to repel fleas and other pests. The regular use of a flea comb is an effective aid. It can be dipped in a bowl of soapy water between strokes to kill the fleas caught in the small tines.

5. Exercise. If the pets don't get natural exercise from running and playing, walk them regularly. Healthy animals have a greater resistance to diseases and insect pests. Exercise is good for the animals and for you.

6. Pet treatment. Apply herbal powders of pennyroyal (for dogs only; don't use on cats), eucalyptus, or rosemary. Ready-to-use growth-regulator products such as Petcor and Ovitrol are also available. For the purists, these are not totally organic products; they are chemical growth regulators.

Diatomaceous earth, a true organic product, is an inexpensive and effective tool. Apply as a dry powder to the pet's fur if an infestation exists. Then back off. Don't use D.E. regularly on pets because it's very drying to their skin.

Citrus oil can also help control fleas. Chop orange skins or cut them into very small pieces, then place in a pan of water (enough to just cover). Simmer 15 minutes. Cool thoroughly. Dampen a soft rag with the mixture and rub onto your pet's fur. Pay special attention to areas that are hard for the pet to reach. Other forms of citrus also work, but oranges seem to work best. Commercial citrus products such as Demize are also available.

7. Indoor treatment. Treat infested carpets with D.E. or boric acid, but don't overdo it. For heavy infestations, spray d-limonene (Demize or Flea Stop) and methoprene (Precor or Ovitrol) on carpets and furniture. Again, these products are not purely organic. Some veterinarian publications now recommend Fleabusters Rx as the indoor treatment of choice for flea control. It is a dry application of sodium polyborate that the makers guarantee will eliminate indoor infestations for a year with one application. Baking soda dusted on carpets will also help.

8. Outdoor treatment. Dust or spray D.E. and pyrethrum on infested areas. Light dusting is better than heavy globs. In liquid sprays, add 2 tablespoons D.E. or D.E./pyrethrum to 1 gallon of water. D.E. is nonselective, so use only as needed, to avoid killing beneficial insects. Concentrate on dark, damp spots where fleas hang out. Like all dusty materials, D.E. can cause problems if breathed heavily. Beneficial-nematode products are now available and are very effective against fleas as well as other insect pests.

Note: Remember, D.E. for pets and horticultural use is not the same as swimming-pool D.E., which has been heated and chemically treated. It does not kill insects and is much more dangerous to breathe because it contains a higher level of crystalline silica than food-grade D.E. Buy D.E. only from your local organic retailer.

You thought I forgot about ticks—didn't you?

The same basic program works for ticks with a few exceptions. Ticks mate on animals, then fall off and lay 1,000–5,000 eggs in the soil and in cracks and crevices. Eggs hatch in nineteen to sixty days, and the larval ticks attach themselves to a host animal, feed for three to six days, fall off, and molt into the nymph stage. Some tick adults can live for more than five hundred days without a meal.

Inspect cats and dogs regularly, carefully checking the ears and between toes. Make close inspections when pets return from woods and other possible tick habitats. Comb to remove ticks, but be careful not to break off the mouthparts of any attached ticks. Remove embedded ticks by gently pulling with tweezers, not your fingers. Clean wounds made by ticks with soap and water and apply an antiseptic to prevent infection. Hydrogen peroxide can be used not only to clean wounds but to also help remove ticks. Turn a bottle of hydrogen peroxide over on the attached tick and it will usually let go.

Confine the pets to specific sleeping areas to reduce the area likely to be infested, and reduce hiding places by caulking cracks and crevices where ticks may hide between blood meals. Vacuum and use D.E. or baking soda in any remaining cracks.

Ticks like to climb, so treat tree trunks, caulk building cracks, and attend to areas up on walls and around windows. Use a crevice tool on your vacuum cleaner to get into all small areas. The contents of the vacuum bag should be destroyed by burning or sealing in a plastic bag.

Cleanliness is critical for the control of both fleas and ticks. Besides keeping the dust and dirt cleaned up, remove loose boards, trash, and other debris that can harbor the various life forms of these pests. It sounds like a lot of work, but it's not if done on a consistent basis. The Natural Way flea and tick program is affordable, it has very low toxicity, and—most important—it works!

It should go without saying, but just in case . . . all the above will work much better if your overall lawn and garden program is organic. With healthy biodiversity, the competition and predation of the microbes, insects, lizards, birds, and other animals provide powerful natural balance—as nature designed.

MOM CALLED 'EM WATER BUGS

It is said that all creatures were put on earth for a reason. Really? What possible purpose could there be for roaches? They eat your food, books, and other possessions, poop all over the place, and sometimes spread disease. It has even been said that if we had a nuclear holocaust, the roaches would live through it without any problem—the roaches and the lawyers, that is. Just kidding. These are disgusting creatures (the roaches) to most folks, but we need to discuss them. Roach control is a five-step process:

1. *Exclusion.* Keep them out of your house. Most roaches like it outside until they get hungry, can't find anything tasty there, and walk in through holes or cracks to feast on the water and food crumbs left from dinner. To stop them, fill cracks in masonry, spaces between trim and brick, holes of all kinds, and spaces around pipes with steel wool, copper mesh, or caulking. Put wire screens in air vents, and stop up any other entryways.

2. *Eliminate cracks.* Fill cracks and crevices inside the house. One of the best weapons against roaches is the caulk gun. Every time you fill in a crack with caulk, you reduce the number of roaches that your home can support. Roaches will not mate unless they are nestled in the security of a very small crack. A ⅛-inch wide crack is too wide for roach comfort. The best roach nooks are no wider than the thickness of several pieces of paper.

3. *Remove cardboard boxes.* Another important way to reduce roach hiding places is to eliminate cardboard boxes. The honeycombed interior of their walls offers miles of tunnels which are perfect hiding and mating places, and the glue on cardboard boxes and on paper sacks is attractive food for these critters.

4. *Keep it clean.* Roaches often live outdoors and come in at

night in search of food and water. Eliminating food and water sources such as dripping faucets, leaks, pet water and food, and dirty kitchens makes your home much less attractive to roaches.

5. Feed 'em a surprise. Once the roaches are in the house, there's a two-pronged attack. Boric acid dusted lightly where the bugs are seen is very effective, but use light dustings. If you can see the material after application, so can the roaches, and you've put out too much. Organic Plus, Insectigone, and other D.E. products also work well. Effective homemade baits can be made by mixing 50 percent sugar and 50 percent Arm & Hammer detergent. This is an extremely low-toxicity control, but it still should be put in bait stations or lids and located in areas where pets and children can't get to it. Stronger baits can be made by mixing 2 parts flour, 1 part boric acid, and 1 part sugar; moisten into little balls or cakes. Add more moisture from time to time to keep them more appetizing. A mix of 4 parts boric acid, 4 parts D.E., and 1 part natural pyrethrum also makes an excellent insecticide for roaches. Always keep all pesticides, even these organic home remedies, away from pets and kids.

CHIGGERS

If in the summer you have to walk through property that's dry and weedy, don't forget that it's chigger time and you need to take a few precautions. First, don't wear shorts—that would be dopey. Second, dust your shoes, pant legs, and socks with powdered sulfur. It's available at any nursery or feed store. Rubbing the crushed flowers of horsemint (*Monarda citriodora*, also called lemonmint) on your clothing will also repel chiggers quite well—not as well as sulfur, but quite well.

Chiggers can be controlled with a broadcast application of a D.E./pyrethrum product and/or an application of granular sulfur at 5 pounds per 1,000 square feet. If you have alkaline soil, the sulfur is also a good soil amendment. If you have acid soil, just don't overdo it. If your property is watered occasionally, chiggers will not be a problem.

ORGANIC TERMITE CONTROL

It is not necessary to use toxic chemicals to treat your home or office for termites. Here's a safer and more effective approach.

The first step is to eliminate wet and moist wood from the house or other affected structures. Subterranean termites don't like dry wood. Check carefully for leaks of all kinds and have them fixed. Installing drainage systems around structures is sometimes necessary.

The next step is to put up physical barriers to prevent termites from entering your house. Cracks in concrete beams and slabs provide access from the ground up into the structure. Fill the cracks with silicon caulking to bar the pests' access.

Sand will make an effective termite barrier. Not just any sand will work—you must use a 16-grit sand (also sold as oo sandblasting sand) to create the barrier. The material can be sharp sand, washed silicon sand, or ground basalt (which is lava rock). Put the sand on each side of the grade beam of the structure. Termites can't get through it. The sand prevents them from building the earth tubes up to the wooden parts of the house. A 6-by-6-inch or smaller trench of sand is effective.

If termite tubes are already visible, break them and introduce beneficial nematodes or ants. Both are natural enemies of termites and quite effective. One benefit of the damaging fire ants is that they like to eat termites. Beneficial nematodes can also be used in the soil around structures and are very effective if the soil is kept moist. Encouraging biodiversity is important—as always. When healthy populations of microorganisms and insects exist, the competition keeps heavy populations of bad bugs to a minimum.

Painting or shellacking exposed understory wood will also deter the pests. Painting the wood with boric-acid products is even better. Two excellent products currently on the market are Tim-Bor and Bora-Care. These materials soak into the wood and give long-lasting protection.

Some exterminators are starting to use these alternative techniques. Many others will soon follow. The public is demanding these least-toxic approaches, partly because of their safety, but also because they work! You might ask your exterminator about the techniques I've mentioned and other low-input controls, such as electronic guns, freezing, and frying the pests with high temperatures.

FIRE ANTS

One reader's comment: "I'm almost totally organic." Another reader's comment: "I only use fungicides on my roses." Another: "I'm completely organic—haven't used chemical pesticides or artificial fertilizers on my plants in three years. All I use is some of these Diazinon granules for fire ants."

I've got bad news for you "almost-organic" folks. You're either organic or you're not. The most common error is thinking that it's okay to throw chemical poison at fire ants. "Well," you say, "I wasn't treating the plants—I was just killing fire ants." You forgot something. Organic programs treat the soil, not the plants. The goal of organics is to re-create healthy, balanced, living soil that will give the plants a balance of nutrition. Chemical pesticides foul up the balance of the life in the soil. Not maybe—for sure! Besides, chemical warfare on pest insects doesn't work. Ask farmers about sweet potato whitefly for instance. The repeated applications of pyrethroids and other chemicals not only killed off all the whitefly's natural enemies, it led to the creation of super bugs that were immune to the poison sprays. Better still, ask anyone using chemical fire-ant control why there are still so many fire ants in the south. If they say it's because not everyone is using the poisons, don't be surprised. Wouldn't it be wonderful if every homeowner and every commercial building manager were dumping water soluble chemical poison on every site in all of fire-ant country? Wouldn't that make for healthy soil and lovely, clean groundwater?

Fire ants are a problem pest—they kill small animals, foul up electric devices, and bite people. Why did God put them on earth in the first place? Beats me, but I'll tell you one thing for sure—they are easier to control with an organic program than with toxic chemical warfare. And we don't pollute the world in the process.

Let me tell you a little about these fascinating critters. Fire ants apparently came originally from Brazil to visit here in America about sixty years ago. They landed in Alabama, liked the scenery, and decided to stay awhile. In the early 1940s, there was only one queen per mound, and the mounds were territorial.

After we, in our infinite wisdom, tried to control them with "better life through chemistry," the ants called town meetings to discuss this humanoid irritation. The decision was made to stop being territorial, allow more than one queen per mound, and start getting along better. Instead of 40 mounds per acre, the ants agreed to allow 250 or more mounds per acre, along with 20 to 500 queens per mound. One giant mound has been discovered that contained 3,000 queens. Multiple-queen mounds are harder to control because all the queens have to be killed or neutralized, since each queen can give birth to 1,500–2,000 ants a day.

So much for their life story. To control the little buggers, the first step is to at least try to be smarter than they are. Here's the plan:

1. To control large, serious infestations, apply Logic or Award at 1 pound per acre. To halve the cost per acre, treat a 15-foot swath, skip a 15-foot swath, treat the next 15-foot swath, and so on. Fire ants will easily travel 7½ feet to get the bait. It tastes good to them. Be sure to apply the fenoxycarb baits, such as Logic, to dry soil. If the soil is moist, the stuff *will not work*. The fact that these products break down so fast in moisture is the main reason they fit in an organic program. They work by causing the queen to give birth to young that never mature. One treatment in the spring usually gives excellent control for the entire year. It takes a few weeks to work, but it *does* work.

2. Treat individual mounds with D.E. and pyrethrum. And yes, there are registered products now on the market. Stir the dry material into the mounds or mix 4 tablespoons into a gallon of water and pour into mounds. You can make your own by mixing 75 percent D.E. and 25 percent pyrethrum. The next-best indi-

vidual mound treatments consist of straight vinegar or soapy water poured directly into the center of the mounds. Sorry, there are no registered products available here.

3. Reestablish biodiversity. Fire ants love large monoculture fields of bermudagrass. They don't particularly like diverse stands of native grasses, forbs, and shrubs. They also don't like other native critters—so stop killing them. Some of the most fire-ant-free properties are those that aren't spraying and broadcasting toxic poisons. Various microbes, ants, other insects, lizards, toads, snakes, birds, and other animals help keep the fire ants in check.

By the way, fire ants do have some good points, so having a few fire ants on the property is not all bad. They control, among other critters, ticks, fleas, chiggers, and termites.

The end of April and beginning of May is usually the ideal time to put out fire-ant baits because the queens are about to go on their nuptial flights. Make sure the ground is dry and rain isn't in the forecast for the following day. For a test, put out some peanut butter, cheese, or tuna to see if the ants are indeed foraging. If they aren't actively searching for food, the baits will do no good whatsoever. If they are foraging, sprinkle the material around the area, but *do not* disturb the mound. If you do, the workers will take the queen to a safer place, and your work will again be wasted. One word of caution: Baits are made to taste good. Use all of the bag, can, or bottle and do not leave unused baits where pets or children can get to them. They are poisonous if eaten right out of the package. Applied lightly around the site according to the label instructions, there will be little or no danger.

Later you can knock out any specific mounds that are left, and that's best done with baking soda, D.E./pyrethrum, or boiling water. To use mound treatments effectively, sneak up on the mound around 11:00 A.M.—seriously. The ants will take the queen deep into the ground if they hear or feel you coming. If they don't hear you, they will have the queen near the surface on the east side of the mound to catch the warmth of the morning sun. I hope I haven't told you so much about these fascinating creatures that you mind scalding or poisoning her to death at this point.

If you have only one or two mounds, buy a gallon of vinegar (preferably 10 percent or 100 grain) and mix in 2 tablespoons of D.E. Pour about ¼ gallon of the mixture into the center of the mound. Do not pour it all over the mound. Vinegar will kill the grass around the mound, and the liquid needs to sink quickly down into the ground through one spot. You'll hear the vinegar hissing and gurgling as it reacts with the soil. Now, stomp the hole shut to seal the gases in the ground. Congratulations! You've just murdered the ants in that mound. If a few get away, don't worry about it—it happens with other products as well.

Since the baits are not yet registered for use in the vegetable garden, here's a tip for you home farmers. Mix 4 tablespoons of a D.E./pyrethrum product (there are several on the market) in 1 gallon of water to form a drench to pour directly into individual mounds. A pump-up sprayer also works well. Stick the nozzle of the sprayer down into the mound all the way to the bottom. It's easy to find the bottom, since the mound itself is very soft and the soil beneath the mound will be harder. Start spraying with the nozzle at the bottom, bring it out of the mound with a circular motion, and finish by spraying the surface of the mound to kill all the little creeps trying to escape. Move fast so they don't crawl up the sprayer and get you. Do not spray the entire garden with this mixture, because it will kill the beneficial insects.

GRUBWORM CONTROL

By midsummer, the chemical pushers will start saying that it's six weeks after the major June bug flight and time to broadcast the diazinon and dursban granules. There are several reasons why that's a bad idea. For starters, most people don't have grub infestations heavy enough to need treatment. If there are only two or three grubs per square foot, there's no need to treat. It's perfectly natural for some grubworms to live in the soil, and some species of grubs don't even damage plants. Few organic gardens have grub problems because the balance of life in the soil usually prevents any one particular organism from becoming a problem. Balance is the key. Grubs found outside the lawn in beds are almost always the beneficial grubs that feed on decaying organic matter. They don't eat roots.

Since I first became involved in completely organic projects, I've seen only two projects with enough grubworm damage to warrant treatment. One project was commercial, the other residential. In both cases the grubworm infestations were merely symptoms of the real problem. Both problem areas were in turf and had fescue grass in shady areas that didn't drain well; in other words, both turf areas were in stress. Organic pesticides such as nicotine sulfate, rotenone, and soaps were used heavily to try to eliminate the problem. In retrospect, I now know that those organic pesticides were not only unsuccessful in stopping the pests, they were actually making the problem worse—they were killing the beneficial soil life. Chemical pesticides would have killed even more of the beneficial organisms in the soil.

An excellent treatment for grub-infested soils is the use of beneficial nematodes, microscopic, nonsegmented roundworms that enter the pest through the mouth or other body opening. Some just drill right in. Once inside the host, nematodes feed, reproduce, and emerge to find new hosts. They can be purchased from insectaries or suppliers, usually on sponges or in liquid form. To apply them, soak in tepid water and pour or spray onto the infested area. After application, the area must be kept moist and cool. Ideal soil temperature is 75–80° F, which in some cases limits the effectiveness of midsummer applications. If you have had a problem in the past, plan to apply the nematodes in early fall or spring. University testing has shown the good nematodes to be very tough and able to stand high temperature. The presence of moisture is critical, however.

Sugar is an excellent treatment for grubs and other soil pests, providing a source of carbohydrates to nourish the microbes that attack them. White sugar works, but dry molasses is better. Either should be applied at 20 pounds per 1,000 square feet and watered in. And no, the sugar doesn't attract ants—not in the soil.

As a final reminder, most seasoned organic gardeners don't need to worry about grubs. The natural populations of fungi, bacteria, parasitic nematodes, and other soil life will control pests such as these. If you see some extremely large grubs, from half-dollar to silver-dollar size, chances are good that you have the larvae of the rhinoceros beetle, an organic-matter eater and a helpful friend.

NEMATODES

Nematodes are microscopic worms that live in the soil. There are good and bad nematodes, and they are very numerous in both healthy and unhealthy soil. Some nematodes eat plant roots, while others eat soil organisms, including other nematodes and insects.

The best-known ones are called "root-knot" nematodes. As they feed on plant roots, they cause cancerous-looking knots to form. Other destructive nematodes live in and eat roots but do not form the knots. They are sometimes more destructive, since they are harder to detect. The symptoms are sometimes a lack of plant vigor and poor growth. When a plant's root system is eaten away, it can't pull the proper amount of water and nutrients from the soil.

When nematodes are a problem, it's a signal that the soil is not in balance and is not full of beneficial life. When soil health is poor, the balance of good and bad microbes is out of kilter. When nature's systems are out of balance, many plants are subject to nematode damage. These plants won't always die, but they will be weak and lacking in flower or fruit production. Many trees, shrubs, and flowers fall into this category, although the amount of damage will vary.

Poor plant selection is the other possible cause of nematode infestation. Unadapted plants are usually in stress because they would much rather be growing in some other part of the world. For example, ajuga groundcover, evergreen euonymus, and boxwood shrubs, when planted in the south, are almost always infested with plant-eating nematodes and other pests.

So, how do we rid the soil of these pests? The answer is, we don't—remember that insects, worms, and other pests are not a problem unless the populations are out of control, out of balance. We can, however, bring them to a naturally controlled population. We can help the balance to return by changing our methods of pest control and fertilization. Use of spray products and fertilizers that stimulate microbial activity in the soil allows a large population of good and bad microbes to exist, and if given the chance, the good guys will win out. Microbes such as fungi, amoebae, and beneficial nematodes will attack and destroy plant-eating nematodes and other harmful pathogens. In other words, the dynamic, natural condition of the soil will control most nematode infestations. All you have to do is stop using high-nitrogen artificial fertilizers and toxic pesticides.

Weeds—Friends or Foes?

What has been the hardest part of switching people's thinking from chemical to organic programs? It hasn't been persuading them to use compost instead of peat moss—anyone who once uses compost properly will never buy peat moss again. It hasn't been getting them to deal with disease problems organically—once they have stopped killing the microorganisms, the beneficial fungi and nematodes control the harmful pathogens. And it hasn't been convincing them of the benefits of organic insect control—the use of healthy sprays, soil improvement, and release of beneficial insects give better pest control than chemical sprays do. No, the toughest part has been changing their attitude toward *weeds in turf*. Many folks have an unreasonable fear or hatred of weeds. Although the use of a comprehensive organic program will eliminate most noxious weeds, some people want more help than that. For those who are bugged by weeds, here's the way it's done organically, starting with some old techniques, then moving on to a new idea.

1. Change your attitude. Don't worry about them so much. Many so-called weeds are wildflowers, herbs, and other grasses that together with turf grasses create a pleasing blend and excellent biodiversity. Monocultures of one type of grass are not natural.

2. Mulch 'em. If you cover all bare soil around shrubs, trees, vines, and other plants with a thick blanket of organic mulch, the weeds will be no more. A thick layer of shredded tree chips, coarse shredded hardwood bark, pine needles, or partially finished compost will eliminate even the toughest weeds. Johnsongrass and bermudagrass will have to be removed by hand the first time through.

3. Mow higher. Raise the lawnmower setting to a minimum height of 2½–3 inches. Taller grass will be in less stress, have deeper roots, be healthier, and crowd out weeds more easily.

4. Do some hand work. Bend over and pull out large noxious weeds when they first begin to appear. Mechanical devices can be purchased that make the task easier. My favorites are "The Weeder," "Weed Popper," and the Lawn Claw.

5. Do not scalp. This spring, save your money and/or time and skip the brainless ritual of scalping the lawn. Scalping does no good but a lot of harm. Mainly, it wastes natural organic matter and exposes the soil to direct sunlight, which dries it out, kills microbes, and stimulates the dormant weed seed to germinate.

6. Do not catch the clippings. No, it's not even okay to catch them and put them in the compost pile. Grass clippings should stay on the lawn. They provide food for microorganisms, help maintain the proper moisture and temperature of the soil, and reduce your fertilizer requirements by about 25 percent.

7. Water correctly. During hot, dry periods, in most situations, 1–2 inches of water should be applied weekly by irrigation. The amount and frequency will vary with climate and soil conditions. The key is to water heavily and deeply on an infrequent basis.

8. Add rock minerals. Twice yearly applications of rock minerals such as granite sand or lava sand at 20–40 pounds per 1,000 square feet will increase the energy, trace minerals, and water-holding capacity of the soil. Lava sand is my favorite.

9. Aerate and use organic fertilizers. Aerate unhealthy soil and apply 100 percent organic fertilizer at 20 pounds per 1,000 square feet. Three applications are needed during the first year of transition from a chemical program. Two applications are usually enough the second year. Aeration is no longer needed after healthy soil has been achieved; if you see lots and lots of earthworms, the soil is healthy.

10. Apply pre-emergent herbicide. No, I didn't flip out or desert my organic principles. There is such a thing as an organic pre-emergent herbicide. It's called corn gluten meal. Let me tell you a little about this old substance with a new use.

In 1986, Professor of Horticulture Dr. Nick Christians and others at Iowa State University accidentally discovered that cornmeal greatly reduced the germination of creeping bentgrass in fungi tests. The cause of the inhibition was uncertain, so several samples of different parts of the cornmeal were tested, including the starch, corn germ, corn fiber, and corn gluten meal. These trials showed clearly that the inhibiting substance was in the protein fraction, the corn gluten meal.

Corn gluten meal affects the root growth of sprouted seeds—in fact it stops root formation. Seeds treated with corn gluten meal developed no roots and died when water was withheld from the soil surface. The next series of tests at Iowa State showed that corn gluten meal is effective at stopping or inhibiting root formation at the time of germination in a wide variety of grasses and broadleaf weeds. Corn gluten meal was then tested for detrimental effects on established grasses. Not only was it found not to damage mature grass, it was discovered that it made an excellent organic fertilizer. (These results have appeared in the annual Iowa Turfgrass Research Report since 1989 under the name ISU EXPERIMENTAL.)

Five natural compounds in corn gluten meal have been identified by Dianna Liu and Bryan Unruh of Iowa State, and it is these compounds that possess the herbicidal characteristics. Others at Iowa State are continuing to look at additional uses for corn gluten meal such as in corn-crop and strawberry weed control.

Does all this represent the discovery of a natural "weed-and-feed" product for lawns and other turf areas? Maybe so—it's at least worth a try if you've been bugged by weeds. Corn gluten meal is 60 percent corn protein and approximately 10 percent nitrogen (N) by weight, so if you do try it, it's best to reduce the use of other fertilizers, to avoid the application of too much nitrogen. It is a byproduct of the wet-milling process and is sold as feed for dogs, livestock, and fish. It is a fine, yellow powder, but can be pelletized for easier application to the soil. Apply it at 15–20 pounds per 1,000 square feet, just before weed germination—usually around the first of March and the first of October in the south. It has about a three-week window of effectiveness, and the timing must correspond with the natural germination time of the weeds. If you apply it too early or too late, you'll have big, tall, healthy weeds. Moisture is needed to activate the material, but extended wet periods can reduce its effectiveness. (These conditions are also needed for synthetic chemical herbicides to work properly.)

It's a bad idea, but if you do choose to use chemical controls, treat less often, cut the rates way down—by at least half—and add liquid humate to the mix. If you choose to go the organic route, spend some extra money or energy on good-quality compost to spread on the lawn, do a little hand weeding, water regularly and thoroughly but not too often, and realize that not all weeds are bad—in fact, some of the wildflowers and herbs are quite beautiful. Dichondra, clover, violets, grape hyacinths, and anemones are among the best.

THE REAL CAUSE OF WINTER WEEDS

If you haven't yet gone through the ritual of subjecting your lawn to pre-emergent chemical weediciding—good for you! Whether or not your decision was intentional, you did the right thing. Fall is the ideal time to let nature work—it's not the time to knock it off balance.

I have a lot of problems with the frequent use of weed killers. I've often complained that herbicides damage and kill the good as well as the bad living organisms in the soil, but the fact is that the pre-emergence products hurt the balance of *all* life in the soil. Lack of herbicide has *never* been the cause of weeds. Weeds were put on earth to help protect weak soil from erosion and to help turn lifeless soil into soil that is full of life. Weeds don't actually like good soil. They result from compaction, improper mowing heights, too much or too little fertilizer, and improper watering schedules leaving soil in stress and susceptible to their proliferation.

Compacted soils are caused by overuse of artificial fertilizers, by foot and machine traffic, and quite often by frequent, low-volume waterings. Severe rainy seasons also cause soil compaction. Compacted soil results in poor water penetration, poor drainage, weak root systems, and weeds. Severely compacted soil can be helped greatly by mechanical aeration, compost, organic fertilizers, and liquid biostimulants. Mechanical aeration and deep root injections work faster than any other technique and can improve plant growth overnight.

Watering problems that lead to weeds can easily be overcome by adjusting the watering schedule. Healthy plants need long, deep waterings that thoroughly soak the soil. However, both soil and plants need to dry out a little between waterings. Three times per week is the most frequent schedule ever needed, and then only in well-drained areas during the heat of summer. During cooler weather, twice a week is usually plenty. During short, cool days, one deep watering per week is enough. There are no hard and fast rules, however; the moisture level of the soil must be regularly monitored and the frequency of watering adjusted. Soil with the proper moisture level will not have very many weeds because the turf grasses and ornamental plants will be favored and will crowd them out.

Fertilizing improperly can also encourage weeds. High levels of harsh, artificial, soluble, high-nitrogen fertilizers damage soil and encourage shallow-growing plant roots. When roots are shallow, plants dry out fast and are easily stressed, weakening their ability to compete against weeds. Organic fertilizers can be applied less often to produce a slow, natural release of plant nutrients to establish a balance in the soil. Fall is an excellent time for an organic soil feeding.

Thatch buildup can also cause stress in lawn grasses and result in weed problems. Guess what causes thatch? Not enough microbial activity to break down the organic matter. The lack of microbial activity results from the use of too much high-nitrogen fertilizer and other chemicals. While leaving the grass clippings is helpful in an organic program, it is thus sometimes detrimental in a chemical program.

For better turf health and fewer weeds, raise the cutting height of the lawnmower. Taller grass is less stressed and has more leaf surface to catch light and manufacture food, and the taller plants shade the ground better to hold moisture, reduce watering cost, and shade out weeds, which need sunlight to germinate and establish. Having taller turf when freezing weather hits is also a benefit, since the taller grass acts as a mulch and provides insulation from freezing temperatures (there are those who will argue this point—but what else is new?). If you don't get to use this tip this year, remember next spring to set the mower at least one notch higher, to at least 2½ inches. The most noxious weeds will be controlled and virtually eliminated by using these simple cultural practices I've explained.

Now, what did all that have to do with not putting down pre-emergent herbicide? I think all herbicides, chemical or organic, hurt all plants, and I know they hurt the living organisms in the soil. If you eliminate the pre-emergent weed killers, your ornamental plants, and even your trees, will be healthier next spring. And healthier plants, along with the changes to cultural practices, will take care of most weed problems. (By the way, if a few weeds pop up, it's still okay to bend over and pull them out by hand. There are no laws against that yet!)

The British have a much better attitude about lawns than we do in this country. We seem to have a fetish for one-plant monocultures of grass, and that in itself is a contradiction of nature. The British definition of a lawn is a mixture of grasses, wildflowers, herbs, and mosses. Remember that next spring when the henbit, oxalis, and wild violets are in bloom. When the neighbors ask what you're going to do about the henbit in your lawn, say, "Enjoy the purple flowers!"

Hold the Herbicides in the Spring

Herbicides probably have their positive side if they aren't misapplied; however, they definitely have some negative points, especially for homeowners:

1. Roots of trees, grasses, and ornamental plants can be chemically "pruned" by herbicides, especially if rains come after a herbicide application. Pre-emergent herbicides are designed and formulated to break down slowly in the soil to kill tiny weed or grass plants as they germinate. A heavy rain will cause the chemical to break down faster, thus giving the roots of desirable plants a strong shot of weed killer. And, by the way—no, they do not keep the weed seed from germinating, as is often claimed, but kill the plant immediately after it sprouts.

If herbicides can kill these visible sprouts, imagine what they can do to microscopic flora such as beneficial algae, fungi, and bacteria. The worst products in this category are the "weed-and-feed" type fertilizers which contain 2,4-D. Even if you use herbicides, stay away from these products. Serious damage to trees has been directly related to this type of fertilizer.

2. Herbicides can sometimes last longer than is desirable and interfere with the germination of vegetable, flower, and grass seed. Chemicals that effectively control annual weeds may also affect the establishment of desirable plants, including turf-grass seedlings.

3. The cost of regularly applying herbicides can mount up to a substantial part of the grounds-maintenance budget. This money can be used much more effectively on improved cultural practices, organic products, and additional plant materials.

4. Chemical herbicides are harmful to humans and animals if swallowed, inhaled, or absorbed through the skin. That's a direct quote from product labels, by the way.

5. As much as 98 percent of the ingredients of some pre-emergent herbicides are inert ingredients, which are not required by law to be identified on the label. Some of the inert ingredients are harmless materials such as calcine clay and water, but others are chemicals such as xylene, monochlorobenzene, ethylene dichloride, and other pesticides.

6. Chemical pre-emergent herbicides can, as stated on the labels, thin out established turf grasses. Golf-course superintendents have found this to be true and to avoid the problem have chosen to lower the application rates or skip years of application.

7. Even though pre-emergent herbicides are touted not to hurt plants but only to stop seed from germinating, the labels of some of the most widely used products contain cautions such as these: "... should not be applied to newly sprigged areas of bermudagrass, St. Augustine," "should not be applied in the spring to turfgrass planted the previous fall," "do not use on winter overseeded grass," "this product is toxic to fish," "... is recommended for use on mineral soils only," "do not apply peat moss to lawn, groundcovers, or established ornamentals before treating with ... ," and other such comments. That last point is quite interesting. I wonder what happens when herbicides are used on compost-rich soils?

Golf-course superintendents may still have to use herbicides to keep greens and tees weed free, but most homeowners can't devote the time and money to the balancing act that needs to follow the application of poisonous materials.

In short, herbicides create a toxic environment for tender roots and microorganisms in the soil. Even though the microbes can eventually break down the chemicals that aren't leached away into the water system, their energy really should be spent on creating and releasing nutrients for plant growth.

Organic Disease Control

During a friendly, although spirited, debate with one of my critics, the subject of untested and unlabeled products came up—again. We were trying to identify the recommendations that

I make that he could agree with. He said he could not agree with the use of D.E., Triple Action 20, or garlic/pepper tea, and definitely not with the baking-soda trick for fungus control. It was great fun to get the last needle in when my opponent's boss, who was listening to our debate, interrupted with the news that he had tried the baking-soda spray for black spot on roses, and it worked!

Baking soda, right out of the kitchen cabinet, mixed with water and a little soap, controls not only black spot on roses but also other plant-disease pests, such as powdery mildew, gray leaf spot, and brown patch.

Although baking soda has been used in Japan and other countries for centuries as a natural disease fighter, this unique use is being researched further in this country by R. Kenneth Horst, professor of plant pathology at Cornell University in New York. His tests on baking soda, conducted over a three-year period on roses at Sonenberg Gardens in Canandaigua, New York, were funded by Church & Dwight Co., Inc., a Princeton, New Jersey, manufacturer of sodium bicarbonate–based products. The tests were done on roses with fungal susceptibility, and the plants were sprayed with various concentrations of baking soda along with either insecticidal soap or oil in water. The soaps and horticultural oils were added as spreader-stickers. To cross check, some of the roses were treated with soap and water or oil and water only to make sure it wasn't the soap or oil doing the work. Those roses were attacked by the fungus.

The fungus was controlled, however, when sprayed with baking soda. The scientists admit they don't understand exactly why the baking soda works so well. One guess is that it has a buffering effect which changes the acidity of the leaf surface. Another theory is that it changes the topography of the leaf surface and "confuses" the fungal spores. Whatever the reason, it works very well and is inexpensive and nontoxic.

The formula Professor Horst recommended to me is 4 teaspoons (about 1 heaping tablespoon) of baking soda (don't overdo it) and 1 teaspoon of either a mild soap (I use Neolife) or horticultural oil in 1 gallon of water. Don't add other sprays or fertilizers to the mix, as they can cancel out the effect. Light sprays on the foliage are more effective than heavy applications.

For more information, contact Dr. R. Kenneth Horst, Department of Plant Pathology, Cornell University, Ithaca, N.Y. 14853, or Church & Dwight Co., Inc., 469 North Harrison Street, Princeton, N.J. 08543-5297.

I Don't Like Organic Pesticides Either

In an effort to trap me, critics sometimes ask whether I consider nicotine sulfate a safe organic product. The answer is yes and no. Yes, it is an acceptable product for use in an organic program because it is made from naturally occurring materials. It's a highly concentrated derivative of tobacco. It biodegrades very quickly, so it isn't a pollutant to the environment. No, it is not a totally safe product; in fact, straight from the bottle, it is a very toxic poison.

Nicotine sulfate is a good example to use to help explain my philosophy of organics. First of all, I have never personally used it, and I recommend its use only as a last resort for extremely hard-to-kill pests. Usually, there are much safer organic insecticides that will kill the problem insect. Second—and this is the main point—I don't like any kind of pesticide. Whether you are using pyrethrum, rotenone, nicotine sulfate, Malathion, Dursban, Diazinon, chlordane, or nuclear waste, there's a common problem—they all kill a larger percentage of beneficial organisms, insects, and other friends than of the targeted pests. I've heard the figures that less than one-tenth of 1 percent of a pesticide actually gets on the targeted pests. Where does all the rest go? Good question. On good bugs, into the air, into the soil, into groundwater, and into other unintended places.

The organic pest controls are certainly better than the chemical ones because they are natural materials, they biodegrade faster, and they don't leave foreign metabolites in the environment; but my goal, besides converting the world to organics, is to eliminate the need for pesticides of any kind. Absolute elimination is probably not possible, but we can get close if the real organic philosophy is adopted. I know I've said it a million times, but let's see it in print once more: Healthy soil produces healthy plants that have very powerful resistance to insects and diseases.

Misunderstanding about Pesticides

I was recently talking to a nursery owner who was really interested in the fertilizer part of organics but still didn't believe in using anything other than chemical pesticides for pests. Well, we are a long way from understanding nature and life and organics when we continue to think the debate is about pesticides. Whether we use Diazinon and Dursban or D.E. and garlic/pepper tea is beside the point.

Those who understand nature and organics don't want to use any pesticides at all, or at the most only as a last resort. The basic idea of having to kill something to control production just doesn't fit into nature's laws and systems, which are all about stimulating healthy life and balance.

Pest control comes from establishing healthy soil and healthy plants. That's apparently a very difficult proposition for people to accept until they have actually experienced it. But it's easy to experience. To see the difference for yourself, establish test plots that treat one area with organic techniques and a very nearby area with the chemical approach. Plants growing in soil that lacks good mineral balance, proper amounts of humus and organic matter, good drainage, and good tilth will be in stress and will attract bugs. It's nature's way. Those plants will have two basic problems, one of which is that they will not have enough sugar. Sugar content can be easily calculated using a tool called a refractometer, or you can also simply use your own taste buds on food crops. The second problem is that those plants growing with high-nitrogen artificial fertilizers will not have the proper balance of minerals. When balance doesn't exist, bugs will regularly attack the plants. Don't take my word for it—give it a try; it's easy to see.

When I have occasional outbreaks of insect pests (every organic gardener, and every chemical gardener, will), I kill the pests, but I use the least toxic method available. I first try to determine what caused the attack of the pest. In most cases the cause is stress. Stress happens in people, in livestock, in small animals, and in plants. It has various causes. One could be that you planted something in Dallas, Texas, that would really rather be living in Seattle, Washington. Another cause of stress is unhealthy soil—soil that's not properly balanced, that's not draining, that is compacted, or that lacks mineral balance. The true solution lies in fixing whatever that major problem is, not just killing the symptoms we call pests. Symptom pests can be killed with organic pesticides which have low toxicity and biodegrade rapidly, but the major problems must be fixed or the pests will return.

The most common insect pests in the spring are aphids on new succulent growth. They can be controlled by the following methods, arranged in order of increasing toxicity from 1 to 7. Try to use the least toxic methods first and increase your weaponry as needed.

1. Release ladybugs after wetting the foliage.
2. Spray strong blasts of water on the infested foliage and release ladybugs.
3. Spray garlic/pepper tea.
4. Spray strong blasts of water with a mild insecticidal soap solution.
5. Spray pyrethrum.
6. Spray pyrethrum-and-rotenone combination products. (If you still have aphids at this point, you need to consider moving.)
7. Dust or spray with sabadilla dust.
8. Move!

I learned a long time ago not to get into the argument about whether or not pesticides are dangerous. Most people have their minds made up on that issue, and I'm not going to change them. All I hope to do is teach people that pesticides simply aren't necessary. Remember that most of the insects in the world are beneficial, and every time you spray a pesticide, whether it's a chemical or organic, you will always be killing more beneficial organisms than targeted insects and diseases.

5 Organic Landscaping

Organic Tree Care

A little book by Shel Silverstein called *The Giving Tree* may be considered a children's book, but it says as much about the value of trees as any words ever written. Trees provide beauty, grace, color, shade, a place for climbing, swings, and hammocks, food for animals and people, screening of bad views and framing of good ones, soil improvement, fuel, lumber, and organic matter for the soil. Try asking that of a gardenia.

Trees are also the first consideration in garden design. They create the framework for all that happens in the landscape. Trees are the only home improvement that can return as much as 100 times the original investment, provided they are chosen correctly, planted correctly, and maintained correctly. Even though the proper care and maintenance of trees is critical, this is the part of landscape maintenance where I see the most expensive mistakes being made.

Even some of my past associates have had trouble fully grasping what I mean by "organic tree care," but it's really quite simple. Nature uses organic or natural techniques, so why shouldn't we? Without artificial treatments and products, tree care can be much more effective and less costly. The secret is to watch how trees are maintained in the wild and attempt to emulate those techniques.

We actually have an advantage over nature in that we can control the environment to a degree by regulating the nutrients and the moisture level. We also can respond more quickly to situations that have gotten out of balance. But it's of no help to beat around the bush—let's get down to some actual tree-care techniques. The following is a list of procedures that I consider faulty. Some are a waste of time and money, others are detrimental to the health of trees, and some are just plain stupid. Let's call them collectively "bad tree-care techniques." Afterward I'll give the procedures that I recommend instead.

Bad Tree-care Technique #1: Overpruning

Removing heavy amounts of limbs and foliage is almost always unnecessary, especially with deciduous trees. It's better to watch how trees of a particular variety grow naturally and then trim your own trees similarly, attempting to preserve each plant's natural character. The height and width of the tree should be left intact. Likewise, the overall mass of foliage should be preserved, and pruning cuts should not be obvious. Cutting limbs off a tree hurts the tree. Heavy thinning and severe opening of a tree's canopy throws the plant out of balance. When a tree is out of balance and in stress, it has an increased susceptibility to insect pests, diseases, and wind and ice damage. Severe pruning and removal of the interior limbs and foliage is appropriately called "gutting." To prune a tree properly, think about balance and maintaining a natural look.

No matter what you have heard from other sources, trees need little pruning at planting time. In most cases, all that is necessary is the removal of broken or damaged limbs and suckers. It's a mistake to thin out the limbs to match the proportion of roots that have been lost. The more foliage that can be left on the tree, the better chance the root system has to redevelop. A few evergreen, field-collected trees, such as yaupon hollies and live oaks, do respond positively to a moderate amount of thinning when transplanted, but deciduous trees need no pruning during planting or transplanting, and container-grown trees certainly need no pruning.

Bad Tree-care Technique #2: Cutting Away Lower Limbs

The main reason the lower limbs of trees are so often cut away is that they are the easiest limbs to reach. The idea that removing lower limbs is good for the health of the tree is, shall we say, misguided. Some people think that removing lower limbs will make trees grow faster and taller. Wrong: trees grow better if more foliage is left in place. I have seen trees die from the stress caused from the excessive removal of lower limbs. Conversely, low-sweeping limbs and branches add to the grace and beauty of a tree while helping to maintain the plant's natural balance.

The only pruning of large trees that I normally recommend is the removal of dead or damaged limbs, limbs that are rubbing or in conflict, limbs with mistletoe or disease, and limbs that are dangerous; in certain cases, I also recommend a light overall thinning to allow shafts of sunlight through the tree to the ground plane below.

Bad Tree-care Technique #3: Making Flush Cuts

Pruning cuts should *not* be made flush with the trunk of the tree. Even though flush cuts are still recommended by people who should know better, all scientific research and evidence indicates that a small stub called the "branch collar" should be preserved, since this is the means by which the wound is naturally healed. Watch how tree limbs are naturally removed in the forest, and you'll notice that the branch collar is always left when the limb falls away.

A proper pruning cut is round and helps the tree to seal off pathogens and protect itself from diseases that might be present. An improper flush cut is oval or football shaped and larger in area, providing disease organisms and insects with a weak wound to attack. Flush cuts can actually cause disease and decay to spread into healthy tissue. Long stubs are also detrimental and should be avoided. Both long stubs and flush cuts delay healing and invite many problems.

Bad Tree-Care Technique #4: Using Band-Aids

Research has shown that pruning paint slows the healing of cuts and may have long-lasting negative effects. It does appear that painting the cuts of oaks in oak-decline areas may have some benefit, but in most cases the painting of pruning cuts is a waste of time and money and slows the healing process.

Nature does not paint cuts when limbs fall from the trees. Just as a cut finger heals faster when exposed to the air, so does a tree wound. Likewise, wound dressings and wraps are wasteful and detrimental. After the freeze of 1983, a great deal of time, effort, and money was spent on wrapping damaged tree trunks. The wrapping didn't help any, but it did cause a lot of problems. Trunk wrapping with burlap or paper only gives insects and diseases a good home. The proper procedure is to remove the loose, broken bark but to leave the damaged spot exposed to the air. Keep the wound clean and uncovered and the natural healing process will work quickly and efficiently.

Bad Tree-Care Technique #5: Excessive Cabling

The practice of holding tree limbs up with metal cables (thick wires) to aid tree structure should have little use in horticulture. If correct pruning procedures are used, cabling is unnecessary, and it rarely has any positive contribution to make. It costs a lot, looks bad, wounds the tree, and only moves the stress point in the tree from point A to point B. Cables are unsightly and create an artificial tension in the tree that can actually lead to more ice and wind breakage rather than less. The only exception is the cabling of upright limbs or trunks which form a weak V connection at their base. The cabling in this case should be parallel to the ground and connect the two upright parts of the tree. The most serious limb breakage I've ever seen occurred in the terrible ice storm of 1979 on limbs growing straight up. Horizontal limbs had little damage because of their strong tensile strength. The point is that most of the cabling I see used is on horizontal limbs and is therefore unnecessary. Under no circumstances should cables be used in an attempt to hold up low-sweeping or horizontal limbs. If those limbs are dangerous, they should be removed.

Bad Tree-Care Technique #6: Treating Only Part of the Tree

The proper care of trees involves much more than pruning the top. Other important procedures include working on the soil and the roots. Remember that, in terms of its health, the most important part of a tree is below the ground. Don't treat the top and forget the roots. At least 50 percent of a tree's life-support system lies beneath the ground. When problems start to show up in the foliage, the damage to the root system may have already gone too far. It's critical to take action as soon as symptoms appear. Most soil problems relate to poor drainage and poor aeration. Sometimes actual drain lines need to be added to eliminate excess water, but in most cases the following procedure will improve the soil's health:

Aerate by punching holes in the ground 4 inches or deeper.

Apply lava sand at 50 pounds per 1,000 square feet.

Apply organic fertilizer at 20 pounds per 1,000 square feet and place a ½-inch layer of compost over the entire root system area.

If the tree is in a bed or bare area, add a 3–5-inch layer of coarse-textured mulch on top of the compost.

Bad Tree-Care Technique #7: Using Chemicals

Trees are the easiest of all plant types to maintain organically. Chemical pesticides and artificial fertilizers throw nature out of balance and allow a vicious cycle of problems to begin. In contrast, organic techniques and products help to keep nature's systems in balance, won't pollute the environment, are safe to people, pets, and wildlife, are fun to use, and work better than chemical programs.

How to Work around Existing Trees

All trees are important in one way or another. Some provide welcome shade, some bear fruit, and all discourage erosion, clean the air, and produce oxygen. Even junk trees such as hackberries are good for the soil improvement. It is very important to be as sensitive as possible to all existing trees, especially when working around them on construction sites.

Some trees are extremely sensitive to "wet feet" in soggy and poorly drained soils. Maintaining positive drainage is extremely important. Healthy soil, positive surface drainage, and even underground drain lines all help. Pecan, live oak, cedar elm, and lacebark elm are usually the easiest trees to work around, although that's not always a sure thing—all trees prefer their roots to remain undisturbed, and they all prefer healthy soil to compacted, dead soil.

Quite often, no effort is made to protect existing trees during the construction of new houses or commercial buildings, and when protective measures are taken, they are usually not very effective. Staying away from the root system and leaving the grade and the surface and underground drainage patterns intact are essential to a tree's health. Although a tree's roots grow out far beyond the edge of the foliage (the drip line), protecting the area from the drip line to the trunk will give most trees a pretty good chance of surviving the disruption caused by construction.

If existing trees are to be retained in a project, and in most cases they should be, the first and most important task of the designer and contractor is to protect the trees from the workers. Protection from stored construction materials, from grade level adjustments, and from all traffic is even more important than protection against physical damage to limbs and trunks.

Since buying new trees is expensive, I recommend you work hard to keep any existing ones alive. Installing a physical barrier such as a wire barricade or fence is the only method that works to keep automobile and foot traffic, fill soil, and construction debris off the root system. Compaction of the soil is often the result of the traffic and the storage of construction materials. When the soil is compacted, air is shut off from the roots and all the natural systems are slowed or shut down.

It's always a fight to keep the contractors and the property owners away from trees. It's usually inconvenient for them not to use the space around the trees. But that's tough! Trees are more important than the contractor's convenience. Substantial monetary penalties will usually get their attention and should be used.

Here are some examples of protective techniques:

Trunk protection. Strap boards (never nail them) to the trunk of trees to protect them from being hit and damaged by construction equipment or cars.

Fences. Temporary chain-link fences are an easy, economical way to protect trees during construction. Fences should be installed as far away from the tree trunk as possible—ideally, at the drip line or farther out—to keep traffic off the root system. Snow fences, wooden fences, or other fencing systems can also be used—anything that will block people's access to the root system of the tree. It's simply human nature to walk, sit, park, have lunch, and store stuff under trees. *Don't let 'em do it!*

Erosion protection. A third protective device is usually used in commercial installations but is good for any project. Filter-fabric fences or hay bales are placed uphill from trees to protect them from excessive water and sedimentation running down the slope. Water washing freely across a tree's root system can cause damage by either washing soil away from the roots or depositing soil on the roots from uphill.

Mulch. A heavy layer of tree chips (8–12 inches deep) can be used as a protective blanket on the ground to protect tree roots from storage of materials, foot and machine traffic, and other sources of compaction during construction. The chips can usually be obtained inexpensively or free from tree-pruning companies that otherwise would have to pay to dump the chips in city landfills. During construction, the chips will cushion the roots, shade the soil, and start to decompose into humus.

A final note of advice to homeowners: *Do not* allow building contractors to prune any tree limbs. Let's just say that such people lack a certain sensitivity. It's always best to hire a professional arborist to trim away any conflicting limbs. Most arborists will also be able to carry out the soil treatments that I have recommended.

UTILITY LINES

Sprinkler, electrical, drainage, gas, water, and sewer lines have to be dealt with on construction sites. Unfortunately for trees, these lines are usually trenched wherever it's the easiest to dig them in. Severe damage is done to a tree by trenching through the root system.

If there's an option, all ditch digging should be kept away from trees; however, in many cases there's no choice. It takes a little thought to handle installing utility lines through an area with trees. First of all, plan where the lines will go and have the path staked out prior to digging. Think about it, and move the path around if necessary to locate the lines where they will do the least damage to the trees. Some utilities can be put together in the same trench, cutting down on the number of ditches as well as the cost. When lines have to be dug through roots, place the trench halfway between the two trees. That keeps the cut as far away as possible from both trees. If one tree is better than the other, favor the best tree.

When you have the option, dig utility lines parallel with roots (radiating out from the trunk) rather than across them. This technique is often possible for night-lighting lines, sprinkler lines, and drainage lines. Utilities that must cross roots should be carefully dug by hand so that major roots can be left uncut and growing through the trenches, and the utility lines placed under them.

An often-asked question is how much of the root system can be cut away without hurting the tree. There's no straightforward answer. Even though careful root pruning is no more detrimental than correct limb pruning, almost any destruction of the root zone stresses the plant. The frequently used rule of staying out-side the drip line is easy to remember but not foolproof.

One thing is certain, however—limiting the damage will always benefit the tree. People who claim that they have worked all around and all over the roots of trees and these trees have lived don't realize that quite often death from construction damage doesn't occur until five to ten years after the damage was done.

People Don't Grow Trees

People don't grow trees—trees grow in spite of people. In some cases people *allow* trees to grow, and in a few rare cases people actually *help* trees to grow. If we people-types give trees half a chance, they will grow well for us and be quite healthy.

There are a few fundamental rules that I have stumbled upon through the years that seem bluntly apparent but have been used little. To put them in a nutshell, choose a tree well suited to your particular soil and climate and plant it in a way that most closely resembles the way it would naturally grow in a forest. Sounds simple, doesn't it? It is!

The very first time I saw trees planted correctly was in 1976. I had been commissioned to design the landscaping for the Harris Corporation on the Dallas North Parkway in Addison, Texas. The budget was tight, and the site was large and uninteresting. I used the excess soil from the building excavation to create free-flowing berms. These mounds added interest to the otherwise boring flat site and provided appropriate places for trees to be planted. Unintentionally, I had created a built-in drainage system as well as a more interesting-looking site. However, what I learned from that project that turned out to be invaluable was how to plant trees correctly. I didn't realize at the time that I had learned the art of planting trees organically.

An old friend, Cody Carter, planted all the trees on that job. Since that time, I've watched those trees, and I've watched trees on other projects that have been planted using various other techniques. Here's what I learned and what I recommend to you:

Dig an ugly hole. Dig a wide, rough-sided hole exactly the same depth as the height of the root ball. Don't guess—measure the ball and the hole as it's dug. The width is a different story. The hole should be much wider than the ball—at least three times as wide, especially at the surface of the ground. (The width of the bottom of the hole is not so important.) The sides of the hole should be rough and jagged, never slick or glazed like those made by a tree spade or auger. Holes with glazed sides greatly restrict root penetration into the surrounding soil and consequently limit proper root development.

Run a perk test. After digging the hole, fill it with water and wait until the next day. If the water level doesn't drop substantially overnight—at least 50 percent of the hole depth—move the tree to another location or add drainage. Tree holes must drain well for proper root development and overall tree health. The drainage is ideal if the water drains completely out of the hole overnight. *Tip:* Add a little seaweed to the water. As the water level recedes the seaweed will soak into the soil, and microbial activity will get a head start.

If the water level in the hole remains stationary overnight, you have a drainage problem, to which there are three possible solutions:

1. Add a drain line made of PVC pipe set in gravel, running from the tree hole to a lower point on the site.
2. Dig a sump or pier hole from the bottom of the hole down into a different soil type, or break into rock. A sump from the top down to the bottom of the root ball is useless.
3. Move the tree to a new location.

Positive drainage is critical, so don't skip this step or cut corners on it.

Backfill with existing soil. Place the tree in the center of the hole and make sure the top of the root ball is flush with the surrounding grade. If it is slightly higher, that's okay, but slightly lower is the kiss of death, as the tree can easily drown. Backfill only with the soil that came from the hole. *I'll repeat that: Backfill* *only with the soil that came from the hole.* Adding amendments such as peat moss, pine bark, sand, fertilizer, or foreign soils to the backfill not only wastes money but is detrimental to the tree. Putting gravel in the bottom of the hole is a total waste of money. When the hole is dug in solid rock, topsoil from the same area should be used. Some of the soil's native rock mixed into the backfill soil is beneficial. Topsoil from the immediate area rather than subsoil should be used for the top 6–12 inches of backfill if possible. Mixing a little compost into the top 6 inches of backfill is okay but not necessary.

With field-dug trees, remove the burlap from the top of the root ball as well as all nylon, plastic string, and wire mesh. Burlap can be left on the sides of the root ball. With container trees, which are usually pot bound, cut or tear the outer roots away from the root ball; don't destroy the earth ball, but do rough up the solid mass of the roots. This loosening of the roots is a critical step in the planting of container trees but should not be done to balled and burlapped trees. After backfilling, settle the soil thoroughly with water to remove all air pockets. Do not tamp the backfill with your foot or with a two-by-four. Let the water settle the soil naturally in the hole.

Bare-rooted plants, balled and burlapped plants, and container plants should all be planted the same way. With bare-rooted plants, it is important to protect the roots from drying during the planting process.

Do not wrap or stake. Wrapping tree trunks with paper or burlap is a waste of money, looks unattractive, harbors insects, and leaves the bark weak when the wrap is removed. Tree wrapping has the same effect as leaving a bandage on your finger too long; like skin, tree trunks need air.

If the tree has been planted properly, staking and guying is usually unnecessary, as well as being a waste of money and detrimental to the proper trunk development of the plant. Staking should only be done as a last resort, and stakes should never be left in place for more than one growing season. Temporary staking should be done with strong wire, metal or wooden stakes, and pieces of garden hose at the tree to prevent injury. Again, *staking should be done only as a last resort.* It is not only unsightly and expensive, it adds to mowing and trimming costs and restricts the tree's ability to develop tensile strength in the trunk. In areas of the country where sunburn on trunks is a problem, applying whitewash made from water-based, nontoxic paint is much better than wrapping. As the whitewash wears off, the bark will slowly adjust to the sun and the ultraviolet rays.

Do not overprune. As mentioned above, it's not true that limb pruning must be done to compensate for root loss during planting or transplanting. Most trees fare much better if all the limbs and foliage are left intact. The more foliage a tree has, the more food can be produced to help build the root system. The health of the root system is the key to the overall health of the tree. The only trees that seem to respond positively to thinning at the time of transplanting are densely foliated evergreen trees such as live oak and yaupon holly collected from the wild. Plants purchased in containers definitely need no pruning when planted. There is strong evidence that severely pruning bare-rooted plants is more detrimental than beneficial.

Mulch the top of the root ball. If the new tree is planted in a grassy area, do not plant grass above the root ball. After the back-fill has thoroughly settled, apply ½ inch of compost across the disturbed area. On top of the compost, add 3–5 inches of coarse-textured mulch such as native tree chips or shredded hardwood bark. The compost will act as a slow-release fertilizer. The reason to avoid grass above the root ball is to eliminate the competition for water, nutrients, and especially oxygen. As the tree becomes established, it's okay for the grass to grow in toward the trunk, although maintaining a mulched area around the trunk of the tree is healthy and helps keep the line trimmers and mowers away from the trunk. Adding some organic fertilizer to the surface of the soil after planting will help the tree become established more quickly.

If you have followed the above techniques, not only have you planted your tree properly, you have re-created the forest floor under it. Why is that important? Remember that all trees, fruiting and ornamental, originally came from the forest. And all forests have compost and mulch litter on the ground.

Summer Tree Care

Trees are easy to maintain, even in the heat of summer. Walk into any forest or wooded area, and you will rarely see anyone fertilizing or spraying for pests. Many natural systems and processes are constantly at work to make trees grow and stay healthy. Nature irrigates the native trees with rain, and the water is preserved in the soil to a great extent by the shade of the trees, but also by the mulch of leaves, twigs, and animal waste that collects on the forest floor. You'll notice that in a healthy stand of native plants, no bare soil will be exposed.

Fertilizer for the forest is the natural compost that is created by the mulch or forest litter. As the soil microorganisms feed on and biodegrade the vegetative and animal waste, fertilizer nutrients are created and released.

How does all that relate to the tree in your front yard? It simply means that it isn't necessary to work hard at maintaining trees in a landscape. Assuming that you have chosen a good-quality tree and have planted it correctly and in a place where it will like growing, little maintenance is needed. What's critical is that you allow nature's systems to function and to keep the plants out of stress. Fertilize your trees with compost (the best choice—just like what's used in the forest without our help) or organic fertilizers such as alfalfa meal, cottonseed meal, earthworm castings, composted manures, or humates. Protect the soil in the root system from compaction or contamination. Give trees extra water only during drought periods; at other times the normal garden watering is enough. Although tree pruning is most often done in the fall and winter, trimming can be done during the growing season if necessary. During the summer dead, damaged, and diseased limbs and foliage can be seen easily. About the only tree problem that's easier to spot in the winter is mistletoe infestation.

Less is best in pruning. It should be done so that when you're finished, no one will be able to tell you did anything. Lower limbs should not be indiscriminately removed, and heavy foliage removal is not only unnecessary but detrimental to the tree's health—limbs or trunks can become sunburned, and the loss of foliage reduces the tree's ability to photosynthesize (make food from sunlight and carbon dioxide).

People who hack up trees by dehorning (severely cutting back) or topping deserve to have *their* arms and legs cut off too. Under no circumstances should severe dehorning of trees be done. Cutting the top off a tree is the worst form of hackery, and the drastic raising of a tree's canopy by cutting away the lower limbs is almost as bad.

Insects are not a big bother to healthy trees. Lots of low-quality trees and a few good trees such as persimmon and pecan are sometimes plagued in the summer by tent caterpillars, but these insects are more unsightly than damaging and can easily be controlled by spraying at the first sign of trouble with Bt (*Bacillus thuringiensis*) sold as Dipel, Bio-Worm, and Thuricide. Bt should be sprayed late in the day to kill the caterpillars as they feed at night. To avoid having to spray even these organic pesticides, protect the populations of native wasps. They love the taste of worms. Trichogramma, a tiny, gnatlike wasp, can be purchased and released. Green lacewings will also help control worms.

Aphids can sometimes be a nuisance on certain trees but rarely cause serious damage. They can be controlled by spraying the trees with water and releasing ladybugs. The reason for the water is that the ladybugs will be thirsty when first released. Put a tablespoon of blackstrap molasses in each gallon of spray to make it more tasty for the good bugs. For best results, do this work early in the morning or around dusk.

Red spider mites attack some trees, especially those in stress as a result of soil problems, but the mites can be controlled by spraying summer horticultural oil or garlic/pepper tea every three days for nine days. The ideal treatment, however—and one that will help greatly in the control of spider mites, aphids, and other small pests such as thrips, is spraying water and molasses and then releasing green lacewings. Green lacewings and other beneficial insects will flourish if all pesticide sprays are eliminated. Garlic spray is an effective preventative if sprayed before infestation occurs.

Spraying liquid organic products on the foliage and on the soil under trees can help to stimulate all the natural systems in the trees and in the soil. Good liquid products which provide micronutrients, hormones, and beneficial microscopic flora and fauna include seaweed, fish emulsion, apple cider vinegar, molasses, and commercial biostimulants.

High-quality trees have few fungal problems, but those pests that they are sometimes troubled with, such as powdery mildew and black spot, can be controlled by spraying baking soda and water mixed at 4 teaspoons (approximately 1 rounded tablespoon) per gallon with the addition of soap or horticultural oil at 1 teaspoon per gallon. Apple cider vinegar at 1½ ounces per gallon of water is another good homemade fungicide.

Don't forget to add 1 inch of compost to the surface under newly planted trees, with at least 3 inches of shredded hardwood bark, tree chips, or hay above the compost. As a final note, watch out for "mower and weed-eater blight." Machine and machine-operator problems are among the leading causes of damage and death in trees.

Fall: The Pruning Season

It's fall, and yes, it's now major pruning season. But before you fire up the chain saw, let's go over some guidelines for organic tree care.

First of all, it's important to understand how a tree grows. Homeowners are often surprised to learn that the root system of a tree grows primarily in the top 12 inches of soil and even more surprised to discover that it stretches out far past the drip line, sometimes reaching two to three times the diameter of the tree foliage. It also comes as a surprise to many people when I say that most pruning is overdone. Trees grow and maintain themselves quite well in the wild without our pruning help. Doesn't it seem sensible that the best approach to pruning should be to try to duplicate nature's techniques as much as possible?

Shade trees, ornamental trees, and decorative understory trees can be trimmed any time of the year, but the most effective time is from fall to spring. Fruit trees, on the other hand, should be pruned only from midwinter up until just before bud break in late winter. This timing is especially critical for certain fruit trees, to avoid the forcing of early flowers which can be damaged by a late frost. Peach trees, for example, should be pruned as late in the winter as possible.

When deciding how to prune a tree, first stand back and look it over carefully. The overall character and shape of the tree needs to be preserved. It's a mistake to think that we can manipulate and change the character and the overall, long-term shape of a tree. It can't be done.

Next, look for the dead wood in the tree. All dead limbs, dead branches, and broken, diseased, or damaged limbs should be removed, as should the weakest of crossing limbs, any limbs that grow into the center of the tree, and limbs that are dangerous or interfere with other activities. Removing limbs just to eliminate a certain percentage of the foliage is a mistake. Pruning cuts hurt trees. Don't do any more than is absolutely necessary.

Here are some guidelines for making the pruning cuts. (These same techniques should be used when removing small limbs from larger limbs.) Use sharp, well-maintained tools. Hand tools such as bow saws, Japanese pruning saws, and loppers are good for smaller limbs. Chain saws can be used for larger limbs, but only with great care and a thorough understanding of the equipment.

Pruning cuts should be made where the branch meets the trunk—that is, a little way out from the trunk. The branch collar, a protective boundary that looks like a small swelling or bulge connected to the trunk of the tree, should never be removed or damaged. The branch collar, which is actually part of the tree trunk, will have the appearance of a small stub after pruning. The branch bark ridge, the scarlike tissue that exists above the branch collar, should also be left intact on the tree. None of the branch itself, however, should be left after the pruning cut is made. If it is left accidentally, it will provide food for pathogens that can later enter the tree.

Flush cuts, which unfortunately are still sometimes recommended, should never be used. Unlike properly placed cuts, which are round and small and heal quickly, flush cuts form large, oval-shaped wounds that encourage the start of cavities. This is not disputed by knowledgeable tree people, to whom it's well known that cutting into or removing the branch bark ridge or the branch collar causes problems. Such researchers as Alex Shigo and Carl Whitcomb have been lecturing and writing about this fact for years.

Shigo blames flush cuts for at least fourteen serious tree problems, including discolored wood (which is a problem in commercial forests), decayed wood, wet wood, resin pockets, cracks, sun injury, and a number of cankers, and claims that they slow the growth of new wood in the area of the improper cut.

Both Shigo and Whitcomb have mentioned that the genus *Prunus*, which includes peaches, plums, and apricots, is particularly sensitive to flush cuts. Many of the fruit-tree problems that we hear about so often, including those related to diseases and insects, can often be attributed to improper pruning cuts. The branch collars on fruit trees are quite distinctive and can be easily seen and protected.

Pruning paint is unnecessary. The natural barriers in the tree will resist pathogens if they are allowed to do their job. If pruning cuts are done incorrectly, no amount of pruning paint will help. If the pruning cuts are done properly, then the wound dressings are not needed. Wound dressings can actually protect and stimulate the growth of pathogens and decay.

Cavities in trees are voids in which fungi have rotted healthy material. They usually start as a result of injury to the skin of the tree. To repair cavities, removing the decayed material is all that is needed. Fillers such as concrete and foam are only cosmetic and can protect pathogens. When removing decayed matter from cavities, be careful not to cut or punch into the living tissue. Such injuries can introduce decay farther into the healthy wood.

When cavities hold water, drain tubes are sometimes inserted to drain the pockets. This, however, is another bad idea, since the drain tubes puncture the protective barrier between the rotted and healthy wood and cause decay to spread. It is for much the same reason that I don't recommend injector systems for fertilizer and insect control.

Other pruning practices that should never be done include topping trees, climbing trees wearing boot spikes, and cutting away lower limbs for no reason. Cabling and bolting are sometimes effective to prevent trees with weak crotches from splitting, but cabling should not be used to hold up limbs. If cables are to be used they should run parallel to the ground and should be installed so that the natural movement of the tree is not completely prohibited. This work can be very dangerous and should be done only by professional arborists.

When pruning has been completed, the limbs that have been removed should be shredded and used to mulch the root systems of the trees or mixed into the compost pile. If you have done your work properly, the trees will not appear to have been pruned.

Saving Sick Trees

If trees have been planted incorrectly, maimed during construction, or maintained poorly, they can go into stress, become sick, and be invaded by insects and diseases.

Can a sick tree be saved? Yes, if the problem is detected early and corrected. It doesn't do any good, however, to eliminate the insect or disease infestation, because these are only symptoms of bigger problems, which almost always relate to the soil and the root system. Often, the damage has gone too far to reverse, but here's how to have the best chance of healing a tree whose health is declining—assuming you've planted an adapted tree. If you have made a bad tree choice, I can't help you.

It's impossible to visually examine the roots of a tree—a live one, anyway, and unfortunately, that's where major tree problems are. Typical diagnostic work usually focuses on the foliage and branches searching for the presence of insects and diseases, but that's the wrong place to look. Pests and pathogens above ground are only symptoms of the real problem—"soil sickness." When soil problems are addressed and solved, tree health improves dramatically, and natural insect and disease resistance resumes. Sick trees usually have one of two soil problems— compaction and poor drainage—and these are often related.

SOIL COMPACTION AND SOIL DRAINAGE

Soil compaction can cause poor drainage and wet soil in some cases and poor percolation and lack of water to the root system in other cases. Healthy soil is loose and rich in living microorganisms and organic matter; it drains well but remains moist for long periods of time. When soil is compacted, the air spaces between the soil particles are so small that little water can be held for use by plant roots.

Poor drainage creates a lack of oxygen in the soil. Water pushes the oxygen out, and when roots do not have adequate oxygen, root respiration slows or stops, and consequently cell growth stops as well. Acids and hydrogen sulfide are created from the anaerobic condition that results, and roots can actually be killed. This damage to root systems often manifests itself in the foliage as wilt, chlorosis, die-back, disease, and pest problems.

Compaction is particularly bad in heavy clay soils, but the problem can be overcome. Some of the best methods for keeping a tree's root system healthy are as follows:

Mechanical aeration. Machines that punch holes can be rented, and most maintenance contractors own or have access to these machines. Holes can be punched by hand throughout tree-root systems in small areas, and in severe cases, post-hole diggers can be used to open air shafts that can then be filled with gravel to create a permanent source of oxygen.

Water injection. Some contractors have soil-injection equipment that blows water under pressure into the root zone of the tree. Water alone will loosen the soil and add oxygen, but fertilizers, root stimulators, and soil amendments can be mixed into the water and injected at the same time at little cost.

Surface treatment with soil amendments. All organic products will help improve soil aggregation (tilth) and therefore improve aeration. Organic products such as compost, liquid seaweed, kelp meal, fish meal and emulsion, and other natural materials will all improve soil compaction and drainage by increasing the population and activity of soil organisms—the microflora and microfauna, microscopic critters that are true friends of the gardener. Rock powders can also help. Some of the best for general soil improvement include lava sand, greensand, colloidal phosphate, and glacial rock powder.

Treatment with living organisms. Biotechnology is currently being developed by many companies, and products containing living microorganisms will become increasingly available.

Preserving the natural soil level. The soil grade should be as close to the original grade as possible. If fill soil has been added to the root zone, it should be removed to allow oxygen to reach the feeder roots. Cutting into the root system is equally damaging. It's important to remember that the most critical roots on any tree are in the top 6 to 9 inches of the soil.

Improving the drainage. Proper drainage isn't an option—it's a must. If a site doesn't drain, trees won't be healthy—it's that simple. Drainage can be accomplished with surface and/or underground solutions. Any system that works is a good system. There are many organic products that will over time improve the physical structure and the drainage of any soil type, but it's still a great benefit to start any project with surface grades and drainage devices that will get rid of excess water as quickly as possible.

Besides making sure that water drains off the surface, I recommend the use of underground drain lines (made from perforated PVC pipe) set in gravel for hard-to-drain areas. Underground drain lines can also help add needed oxygen to the root zone.

Protecting the root zone. During the construction of a new project, *fence off the trees you want to save.* Without a physical barrier, there will be soil compaction from foot, car, and equipment traffic and damage to the sensitive feeder roots that grow in the topsoil. It's equally important to protect the trees from paintbrushes being cleaned out, stored materials, and anything else that could contaminate the soil. Without fences, the trees will be damaged; unfortunately, it's human nature to park cars and store building materials under trees. *Don't let it happen!*

Feeding the soil. Oxygen is the most important and most overlooked nutrient, and introducing air into the soil is, therefore, essential. Apply a product to the root-zone area that will loosen compacted soil by increasing microbial activity. Good choices include fish emulsion, liquid seaweed, liquid humates, molasses, vinegar, hydrogen peroxide, and other organic products. Avoid using harsh chemical fertilizers. Sometimes mechanical aeration is first necessary to speed up the process.

Mulching the root zone. Mulch the entire root zone with a thick layer (3 to 6 inches) of organic material. It's best to use a thin layer (½ to 1 inch) of compost against the soil and then add shredded wood chips or shredded bark on top. The compost at the ground level will help feed the tree, while the heavier material on top will physically protect the roots from traffic, drying, and compaction from rain. This re-creation of the forest floor is the ideal solution, but any mulch at any thickness will help. Don't pile the mulch against the trunk, but do extend it out well beyond the drip line.

Foliar feeding. Spray the foliage with a mixture of fish emulsion, seaweed, molasses, and vinegar. These products stimulate root and top growth in trees that have serious insect or disease trouble.

Broken or damaged bark. Remove the loose, broken bark, but don't wrap the damaged spot. Wrapping only gives insects and diseases a good home. Watch how nature takes care of damage and follow that lesson. Keep the wound clean and exposed to the air, and the natural healing process will work quickly and efficiently.

Remember that the most important part of a tree is underground. Don't treat the top and forget about the bottom. At least 50 percent of a tree's life-support system is below ground level. By the time problems start to show in the foliage, the damage to the root system may have already gone too far, so take action as soon as symptoms appear—or, better still, *before* they appear.

Tree Hacks and Conmen

A reader recently asked my opinion about advice he got from an "arborist" who had recommended a curious solution for the reader's sick red oaks. The diagnosis was "oak decline" and borers. The solution was to spray to cure both.

The trouble is, "oak decline" doesn't mean anything. Trees can decline for a variety of reasons, including soil compaction, root damage, overwatering, winter stress, and contamination from chemical pesticides and artificial fertilizers. None of these applied in this particular instance, which was actually a case of oak wilt. Oak wilt is the proper term for the devastating oak disease that is taking its toll on live oaks and red oaks in the south, and its symptoms are clear—namely, quick and severe die-back as a result of a fungus that clogs the vascular system of the trees.

This tree guy's suggested cure—spraying pesticides—was even worse than his diagnosis. No pesticide spray has even the slightest effect on oak wilt, so if someone recommends spraying to control this disease, don't walk away—*run.*

The death of trees from oak wilt is a serious problem. Oak wilt attacks red oaks, pin oaks, blackjack oaks, water oaks, and live oaks. Trees of the white oak family, such as chinquapin, bur, white, and post oak, seem to be resistant to the disease. To help ailing oaks, apply compost to the root zone and wash it into the soil with a pipe connected to a hose or other soil-injection system. Increasing the air and the humus in the soil will increase the resistance of any tree to any disease. Trenching to separate root systems can help slow the spread of the disease. The only really effective controls, however, are removing infected trees and dramatically improving root systems.

A product called Alamo has been promoted as curing oak wilt, but it is extremely expensive, the process of applying it is laborious, and the results are questionable. According to Larry Schaepveld of the Texas Forest Service, however, it might be worth the trouble and expense to use Alamo on a prize tree, especially if it is close to an infected tree but not yet showing symptoms.

The recommendation of the "arborist" to spray for borers was also ridiculous. His borer diagnosis was made from black spots on the leaves. But borers don't attack the leaves; they bore holes in trunks and limbs. Spraying for borers, even if they *are* present, is a waste of money and a good way to pollute the site. When present, borers in trees can be killed by applying an organic pesticide such as pyrethrum or quinine into the holes and sealing the holes with wood putty. But the only long-term cure for borers is to relieve the stress on sick or ill-chosen trees by improving the health of the soil or to buy tougher trees.

The lesson here is obvious: When hiring a tree-care company, be careful. There are some excellent professionals and some world-class hacks in the business. Get recommendations and interview more than one company. Sources of good advice include the Forest Service and the International Society of Arboriculture. The arborist who recommends doing the least to your tree is usually the best choice. If he or she suggests improvements to the tree's root system, you're on the right track.

Happy Trees—Thanks to Microbes

Thousands of totally organic programs of many different kinds now exist in the United States. What they all have in common is that no artificial fertilizers or toxic chemical pesticides are used. There is another common thread, too: Organic projects have the happiest trees.

The cause of this arboreal euphoria is a group of microscopic organisms called mycorrhizal fungi, or fungus root. From what I've said so far, you know that reestablishing the microscopic life in the soil is a major part of the organic program, but these particular microbes are special. Mycorrhizal fungi are almost always found in the immediate vicinity of plant roots, in the area called the rhizosphere, and they have a very powerful symbiotic relationship with the roots of higher plants. Some of these tiny organisms cloak the outside of root hairs, while others actually grow into the cells of the roots. In both cases these fascinating microbes become part of the root system, making it bigger, stronger, and more efficient.

The benefits of this natural symbiotic relationship are many. The roots provide a nutritional substrate for the fungi and a supply of carbohydrates. The mycorrhizal fungi provide plant roots with the following:

Increased nutrient uptake. Mycorrhizal fungi increase the length and mass of the roots. The result is a greater ability to absorb nutrients. The mycelium mass of the fungi can be as much as one million times the size of the root mass. Mycorrhizal fungi can also act as biochemical intermediaries and convert nutrients to more available forms.

Drought resistance. Mycorrhizae in the root zone increase the root surface area of the plant and expand the amount of soil that it is able to access. Mycorrhizae also increase drought tolerance both for new tree seedlings and for established trees.

Disease protection. Mycorrhizal fungi have been shown to protect seedling roots and mature tree roots from soil-borne diseases. Although less widely appreciated than other benefits, disease protection may be one of the most important reasons to protect and encourage mycorrhizae in the forest, in landscape beds, and in nursery stock. Disease problems are simply microbiotic life that's out of balance. When the beneficial microbes are alive and plentiful, most pathogens are kept in check.

Better establishment of transplants. One of the most widely acknowledged benefits of mycorrhizae is increased survival and growth of newly planted trees, resulting from quicker root growth, larger root systems, and increased disease resistance.

Faster growth. If a plant's root system is healthy, the plant will be healthy. That's a good rule of thumb for all species, and it's especially true for trees. When the roots are healthy and extensive, the top of the plant will be vigorous and pest free.

On all the organic projects I have seen or have been involved with, after the first few weeks of the program's initiation, there has been a dramatic increase in the health of the trees. If you ever have the chance, look at the trees on such Texas-based projects as Frito Lay's national headquarters in Plano, Johnson and Johnson Medical's office facility in Arlington, and Collin County Community College in Plano. These trees have dark green color and more vigorous growth than most chemically maintained trees.

A dramatic example of the power of mycorrhizal fungi is a ginkgo tree in my own landscape. Ginkgo trees are well known as graceful deciduous trees with brilliant yellow fall color on lovely, fan-shaped leaves. Among the oldest trees in the world, they grow on every continent and in almost every soil and climate. Ginkgo is an herb, whose extract may offer brain-metabolism benefits. However, the most widely know fact about the ginkgo is its notoriously slow rate of growth. Gardeners and landscapers have come to expect no more than 2 to 4 inches of growth a year. My little ginkgo was planted as a 1½-inch-caliper tree in 1985. As expected, it grew slowly for the first three years. Then, in 1988, I went completely organic. Since then, a dramatic transformation has taken place. As the soil health increased, the earthworms and microbes flourished, and so did the ginkgo. Each year since 1990, I have measured 18 to 24 inches of new growth. At the end of 1993 the caliper was over 10 inches, and the tree was 33 feet tall. Most trees respond in a similar way to the organic program.

How do you grow these beneficial microorganisms—especially the fantastic mycorrhizal fungi that cause dramatic increases in tree health and growth? All you have to do is bring the soil to life. First, put an end to use of artificial fertilizers and chemical pesticides. Next, to add air, aerate the soil throughout the root zone. Next, raise the humus level in the soil by adding compost and 100 percent organic fertilizers. Last but not least, mulch the roots. Cover all bare soil with a thin layer of earthworm castings, then a ½–1-inch layer of compost, and finally a ¾-inch blanket of shredded hardwood bark or other coarse-textured organic mulch. Don't use filter fabrics or plastic sheets, or the natural processes will be blocked. For an additional push, apply sugar or dry molasses and lava sand, both at the rate of 20 pounds per 1,000 square feet. Within a short time you should have a nice crop of beneficial fungi on the roots of your trees.

Organic Annual Flowers

Everybody loves flowers. Even though flower color in the landscape can be expensive and fairly short-lived, the impact of large, colorful annual beds is wanted by most homeowners and commercial property owners.

An annual is a plant that reaches maturity in one growing season. Within one year or less, the seed germinates and the plant grows, blooms, sets seed, and dies. Plants that have to be replaced each year are also referred to as annuals. Such plants may be tender perennials or tropicals that for various reasons, primarily climate, will not become permanent outdoors.

One of the great benefits of organics is the fact that virtually all plants can be planted in the same kind of beds. Flowers need healthy, balanced beds, as do trees, shrubs, and grasses. "Healthy" beds are created by mixing compost into the existing native soil. Even better beds can be made by adding rock minerals and organic fertilizers. If you put these simple basic elements in place, nature will do the balancing for you.

Here's how to do flower planting in a way that is most effective and gives the greatest chance for success:

Site selection. Annuals are used primarily for show and for cutting. Beds can be used for both purposes, but if they are separate, put the landscape beds where they can be easily seen (front yard, pool area, etc.) but locate the cut-flower beds in utility areas, such as by the driveway or dog run. Easy access to the beds and hard surfaces to walk on are important in maintaining and being able to cut these flowers.

Some flowers, such as impatiens and caladiums, like shade, but most annuals need at least a partial day of full sun. Morning sun is best, and all but the heat-loving choices such as lantana, copper plant, periwinkle, and marigolds like some protection from the hot afternoon sun in warm climates.

Bed preparation. If grass exists, remove a 2-inch layer by hand or with a sod cutter in order to strip away the stolons and rhizomes from which grass can regrow. Add 6 inches of compost, lava sand at 40 pounds per 1,000 square feet of bed area, and organic fertilizer at 20 pounds per 1,000 square feet. If dealing with bare soil, omit the excavation and simply build the bed up. Raised beds are always better than those dug into the ground. Walls can be used for taller beds but aren't needed for slightly raised beds. If you choose to use walls, use concrete or stone; avoid wood, especially the chemically treated kind.

If this sounds simple, that's because it is. Not only is the addition of washed concrete sand, sandy loam, high-nitrogen fertilizers, and other foreign amendments an unnecessary expense—such products can be detrimental to the soil condition. Concrete sand has little to no mineral value and can cause the soil to become concrete-like. Sandy loam has similar problems in addition to being a major source of nutgrass. High-nitrogen fertilizers add too much nitrate and salts to the soil; they also kill our little microorganism and earthworm friends.

Please don't underestimate the exceptional value of compost. Other organic materials aren't even in the same league. Any compost, whether homemade or commercially made, will grow plants much better than pine bark or peat moss.

Pots. To grow flowers organically in pots, use a potting soil that contains compost and other living products. Many of the potting soils on the market are basically sterile, containing only inert materials such as peat moss, bark, perlite, vermiculite, and chemical fertilizers. While organic potting soil has some of the same inert materials, it also includes a high percentage of compost, earthworm castings, and other living materials that contain living microflora and microfauna.

Planting in beds. First of all, wet the bed prior to planting, especially in the summer months. Installing small plants in dry soil can cause desiccation and death. Annuals are usually planted from 2¼-inch or 4-inch pots and sometimes from 1-gallon containers. New plants will often be pot-bound. The solid mass of roots should be cut or broken loose from the tight bond. Don't bare-root the plant, but don't be afraid to rough up the roots a little. Loosening the roots will allow them to grow out more quickly into the beds and establish faster. Small plants should be planted with the top of the root ball flush with the ground but with a slight amount of bed material over the ball.

Each plant should be watered carefully to make sure that the roots are thoroughly saturated at planting. A little bonus you can give to small transplants is a half handful of soft rock phosphate or earthworm castings thrown into each planting hole.

If you are planting seed directly into the garden, soak the seeds first in a 10 percent solution of seaweed or other biostimulant and plant them in bare soil at a depth equal to double the width of the seed.

After plants are installed, the bare soil should be mulched. Any mulch is better than nothing, but the quality does vary. Coarse mulches or rough-textured compost are the best choices because they allow air to circulate down to the soil. Shredded hardwood bark and shredded tree chips are my favorites, but other good choices include cypress mulch, hay, and ground-up leaves. Small-to-medium-sized pine-bark mulch is the worst choice, because not only does it seal off the air from the soil if it stays in place, but it usually blows or washes away, which is an even worse problem. My favorite method is a little more trouble but the results are fantastic! First, put down a ½-inch layer of earthworm castings, next add a 1-inch layer of compost, then finish the surface with a 2-inch layer of shredded hardwood bark or tree chips. This method comes close to duplicating the forest-floor cross section.

Maintenance. If you have an outbreak of aphids, feed them to some ladybugs. If you need to spray an organic pesticide, add some seaweed to the mix for a little extra root stimulation.

Annuals, if planted properly in a mix of compost and native soil, don't need much fertilizer to grow and bloom well, since the compost itself acts as a slow-release fertilizer. However, for quicker response and for more and larger flowers, organic fertilizers can be added. They can be used once per season or, for maximum benefit, as often as every two weeks. Products that work well for annual-flower fertilizers include: earthworm castings at 20 pounds per 1,000 square feet, bat guano at 10–15 pounds per 1,000 square feet, fish emulsion at 2 ounces per gallon per 1,000 square feet, fish meal at 20 pounds per 1,000 square feet, cottonseed meal at 20 pounds per 1,000 square feet, blood meal at 20 pounds per 1,000 square feet, or any of the granulated 100 percent organic fertilizers at 20 pounds per 1,000 square feet.

My own favorite program consists of blending up a witches' brew of several things—earthworm castings, bat guano, and fish meal (each at 20 pounds per 1,000 square feet) once a month, plus a monthly liquid spray application of the following mixture: seaweed at 1 ounce per gallon of water, fish emulsion at 1 ounce per gallon, molasses at ½ ounce per gallon, and natural vinegar at ½ ounce per gallon. By the way, I spray everything else in my garden as well whenever I do this. If you have time, add 1 tablespoon of natural vinegar such as apple cider vinegar to each gallon of water when watering the flowers. This is especially helpful if they are in pots.

Planting Perennials Organically

Irises, daylilies, and yarrow are called perennials because they are permanent. Although most will generally freeze down to the ground in the winter, they return each spring with lush foliage and inspiring displays of flower color. Some perennials are evergreen in the warmer regions of the country.

What you will love about growing perennials organically is that the plants will grow and flower quickly and be much easier to maintain. It's a pleasure to plant and divide perennials in soft, loose, friable, rich, crumbly soil, as opposed to digging around in clay, rock, and hardpan dead soil.

My recommendation for what perennials to use in the landscape is to plant what pleases you. I tend to like large masses of the same plant to make a dramatic impact, although mixes and small, surprising splashes of color in the garden can be very pleasant. Since I am always experimenting, my gardens have a little of everything all over the place, and I'm constantly changing plant types and arrangements to look at new ideas. It's great that perennials can be moved around so easily.

Preparing perennial beds correctly the first time allows the plants to establish more rapidly, grow faster, stay healthier, and bloom more profusely—which is the whole purpose of planting flowers. When the soil is not prepared properly, gardeners are quickly frustrated with the lack of results, and either give up gardening or spend huge sums of money ripping out the plants, re-preparing the beds, and replanting. To save some time, money, and aggravation, give the following method a try:

Remove weeds & grass. Excavate the beds to the depth necessary to remove all weeds and grass, including rhizomes. About 2 inches deep is usually sufficient. Digging out the roots is unnecessary, since grass can only rejuvenate from rhizomes and stolons (below-ground and above-ground stems). Don't use herbicides to kill grass and weeds. Undesirable plants must be dug out whether they are green or brown, so save the money and avoid the chemicals. Remember that our purpose is to create a healthy soil and that herbicides kill plants—both the large ones and the microscopic varieties in the soil. If the soil is bare, don't excavate.

Add native topsoil. If needed, add native topsoil to raise beds to the proper height—to within 2 inches of the adjacent finished grade. Avoid foreign, unnatural materials. Don't add soils different from your native soil, since this can cause a drainage problem by creating a trapped water table. If you need sand, use granite or lava sand.

Add compost. Cover the areas to be planted with a 6-inch layer of properly composted, multi-ingredient organic material—in other words, compost. There are many good commercial composts available but I recommend you use at least some of your own homemade compost together with the store-bought stuff. If you have the space, raw materials, and time, use your own product exclusively.

Add minerals. Most clay soils have plenty of minerals which will be released when you go organic and thus increase the organic matter in the soil, but in most soils the addition of granite sand, greensand, lava rock phosphate, or colloidal phosphate can be beneficial. These rock powders not only help the structure of the soil but also provide food for microorganisms as well as a supply of nutrients. Sandy soils are usually deficient in everything except sand, so it is usually necessary to add mineral supplements to them more often.

Add fertilizer. A light application (10–20 pounds per 1,000 square feet) of a 100 percent organic fertilizer should be broadcast onto the planting bed prior to tilling. Application of a liquid biostimulant is also beneficial.

Till compost together with native soil. Till the compost and the existing topsoil and supplements together until the depth of the compost/soil mixture is 8–10 inches. Tilling deeper is a waste of money and can be detrimental, since driving the organic matter deeper into the soil creates anaerobic breakdown because there's not enough oxygen at that depth.

Raise the beds. The beds should be flat on top and higher than surrounding grades, with their edges sloped for drainage. A small trench at the base of the bed edge helps hold the mulch in place and aids drainage. Walls usually aren't needed for these gently raised beds.

Moisten beds before planting. Planting beds should be moistened before the planting begins, since the young roots of any plants, especially small ones, can dehydrate quickly in dry soil. A key to plant health is to avoid stressful conditions from the very beginning.

Choose your plants. There are many wonderful perennials to choose from. Try some of the following plants for the highest success rate. Consider aster, chrysanthemum, columbine, coreopsis, lily, obedient plant, phlox, Turk's cap, daffodil, dianthus, daisy, iris, purple coneflower, salvia, thrift, verbena, and yarrow. These are just some of the great perennial choices; try others as well. You will be amazed how many different kinds of flowering plants do quite well in your area if given a proper planting bed.

Set the plant properly. Cut or tear pot-bound roots and plant perennials so that the top of the root ball is even with the surrounding soil. The same applies when transplanting divisions. Setting the plant too low may cause deprivation of oxygen and drowning, while planting too high can cause the crown and upper roots to dry out. Spraying the roots of plants with a 5 percent solution of Agrispon, Medina, or some other biostimulant before planting will increase root development.

Mulch beds after planting. A layer of organic mulch at least 3 inches deep should be tossed on the soil after planting. Good mulch choices for perennials include partially finished compost, shredded cypress, shredded hardwood bark, and shredded tree chips.

Divide the plants. Perennials should be divided every few years in order to produce more flowers and more plants, which can be shared with others or used to expand the perennial beds. Division also helps in maintaining a neater, more organized look, which is more important to some gardeners than to others. Some gardeners like a wild look, while others like their planting a little more structured. Division is best done in the cooler parts of the season, and, like pruning, it should be done in the season opposite the bloom season.

Deadheading, the removal of spent blooms, can be done for cosmetic reasons. In addition, severely cutting back perennials right after the heavy flush of blooms starts to fade will stimulate another round of flowers. Toss spent plants and cuttings into the compost pile.

Wildflowers

Wildflowers are now gaining in popularity for use in private and commercial gardens. However, many people become frustrated trying to establish wildflowers. Although growing them can be fairly easy, it isn't as simple as throwing seed out on the ground and hoping nature will do the rest. We need to watch how nature does things and try to use those techniques or even improve on them where possible. Here are some tips for successful wildflower establishment:

Timing. It is better to sow the seed in late summer than at the traditional time in October or November. Late summer is when nature drops the seeds to the soil.

Soil preparation. Begin by raking or lightly disking bare soil to a depth of no more than 1 inch. Deep tilling is a waste of money and is not beneficial for wildflower establishment.

If there is grass in the planting site you've chosen, set the mower on its lowest setting and scalp the area down to bare soil, then lightly disk or aerate the area. Be sure to put this excess vegetation in the compost pile, but remember that grass clippings should always be mixed with other organic ingredients in order to keep the compost pile aerated.

Planting. Mist the seed or, even better, soak it in a 1 percent solution of Medina, Agrispon, or seaweed prior to planting. Let the seed dry, distribute it uniformly over the area at the recommended rate, and rake it lightly into the soil to assure good soil/seed contact. Although not essential, it is ideal to broadcast a ¼-inch layer of compost over the seeded area.

Water the seeded area thoroughly but carefully to avoid eroding the loose soil and displacing the seed. Many of the wildflower varieties will germinate in the fall, and the small plants will be visible all winter. Others will make their appearance the next spring.

Maintenance. The most critical step in wildflower planting is to help nature with the watering if needed. Be sure to provide irrigation (it can be temporary irrigation) the first fall if there is a dry season, and again in March and April if it's an unusually dry spring. The tiny plants need moisture as they germinate and start to grow, although they will survive in low water settings once they are established.

The only fertilization I recommend is a light application of earthworm castings or compost after the seeds, germinate and begin to grow in the early spring, and this is optional.

Selection. Some wildflowers are easier to grow than others. The following are good choices for the beginner:

Gold yarrow *Achillea filipendulina*
White yarrow *Achillea millifolium*
Purple coneflower *Echinacea purpurea*
Coreopsis *Coreopsis lanceolata* yellow and *C. tinctoria* red
Mexican blanket *Gaillardia aristata* and *G. pulchella* red and
    yellow
Gayfeather *Liatris pycnostachya* purple
Lemon mint *Monarda citriodora* purple
Evening primrose *Oenothera* spp. multicolors
Mexican Hat *Ratibida columnaris* yellow and red
Black-eyed Susan *Rudbeckia hirta* yellow

Check with some of the locals for additional choices.

Organic Roses

Yes, you can grow organic roses. Start by selecting those varieties that are the most resistant to problems. Try to avoid roses that develop severe cases of black spot and powdery mildew while you're driving home from the nursery. This is just plain common sense and applies even to those who still insist on spraying toxic chemicals. There are some tough hybrids, and almost all of the antique roses are easy to grow.

Next, plant the roses in well-prepared soil that is a mixture of native soil and compost—lots of compost. The top 8–10 inches of the finished bed should consist of at least 80 percent compost and no more than 20 percent native soil. You can get away with a higher percentage of soil if you are lucky enough to have sandy, acid soil. Raised beds are also a great help, to provide positive drainage and aeration. Retaining walls are optional, since mounding created by adding lots of compost will provide a naturally raised bed.

For those of you who skipped the proper-bed-preparation step and already have roses planted, here are your instructions:

On top of the beds, apply 3–4 inches of compost and 40 pounds of lava sand, or 20 pounds of greensand, per 1,000 square feet and then inject water into the ground around the rosebushes, using a piece of PVC pipe attached to the end of a garden hose. This water injection will both aerate the poorly prepared soil and wash some of the compost down into the ground, but be careful not to wash the roots too heavily. Landscape contractors can provide this service if you don't want to fool with it.

After you have finished the shallow-root injection, apply a 100 percent organic fertilizer such as cottonseed meal or fish meal at 10 pounds per 1,000 square feet and water again to wet the fertilizer. It would be ideal to water the roses again at this point, using a watering can and adding any or all of the following: Epsom salts at 1 tablespoon per gallon, natural vinegar at 1 tablespoon per gallon, and alfalfa meal at ¼ cup per gallon. If you use any one of these materials, there will be an improvement; if you use all of them—stand back!

Next, mulch the bare soil with a thick blanket of alfalfa hay, shredded tree trimmings, or shredded hardwood bark. Don't use pine-bark mulch or synthetic fabrics. Pine bark won't stay in place, and synthetic materials eliminate the natural decay process at the surface of the soil.

For on-going maintenance, spray the foliage every two weeks with a mixture of fish emulsion at 2 tablespoons per gallon of water and liquid seaweed at 1 tablespoon per gallon. Spray occasionally with Epsom salts and apple cider vinegar (each at 1 tablespoon per gallon of water) to darken the foliage color and increase bloom production. Garlic/pepper tea is always helpful, too. Use garlic tea without the pepper if no insect pests are present. Finally, put 1 tablespoon of natural vinegar in each gallon of the irrigation water when possible.

At the first sign of black spot and/or powdery mildew, spray with 4 teaspoons (1 rounded tablespoon) of baking soda plus 1 teaspoon of liquid soap per gallon of water. Spray the foliage lightly but thoroughly. Repeat every five days if the problem persists. Some organic gardeners like to use 1½ ounces (3 tablespoons) of natural vinegar per gallon instead of the baking-soda spray. Both brews are effective natural fungicides.

To control aphids, check the foliage closely to see whether the beneficial insects are taking care of business for you. If the good bugs aren't yet controlling the bad bugs, give the infested leaves a quick blast of water or garlic tea and release some ladybugs and/or green lacewings.

If you feel you *must* "spray to kill," use garlic/pepper tea. The strongest organic pesticide for aphids is a blend of pyrethrum and rotenone, available under several brand names, but I see no need to use these strong products on aphids. Remember that even organic pesticides kill more beneficial organisms than pests.

Landscaping with Herbs

Herbs have been grown for years for their culinary and medicinal uses, but now there's increasing interest in another use—

as landscape plants. While in school, landscape architects aren't taught much about these wonderful plants, yet most herbs are drought tolerant, grow in almost any well-drained soil, and provide color, texture, fragrance, and taste. In addition, they can help with insect control and make excellent companion plants for vegetables and ornamentals. In short, herbs are great choices for organic gardens. Anyone who sprays toxic pesticides on herbs is ignoring the fact that people like to pinch, smell, taste, and eat them fresh out of the healthy soil. Moreover, pests don't bother herb plants. Even if your herbs are only to look at, pesticides aren't needed to maintain them.

There are many different forms of herbs, including bush-type herbs such as salvia and rosemary, excellent groundcovers like oregano, lamb's ear, creeping thyme, and pennyroyal mint, beautiful flowering varieties such as yarrow and Texas tarragon, and trees such as ginkgo, bay, and redbud. The following are some of my favorite herbs to use as landscape plants—which is not to downplay their medicinal and culinary uses—it's just that I wanted you to know about their other uses.

Bay (*Laurus nobilis*). This slow-growing evergreen needs protection from freezes. I grow it in pots and move it inside during harsh weather.

Basil (*Ocimum* spp.). There are many varieties of purple and green basil, and they all make excellent annual plants to use as borders or low masses. Basil will freeze easily, so plant after danger of frost, from seed or from transplants, in sun or partial shade. It will usually return from seed but should be used as an annual in all parts of the country.

Borage (*Borago officinalis*). This is a beautiful, drought-resistant herb that grows to about 3 feet tall. It has gray-green leaves with whitish bristles and star-shaped blue flowers that bloom throughout the summer. Plant in sun or partial shade.

Catnip (*Nepeta cataria*). A tall groundcover or shrubby perennial herb with gray-green oval leaves, catnip grows to 3 feet in height and has small white or lavender flowers. It is excellent for borders and rock gardens, as well as for attracting bees and butterflies—and sometimes cats. Plant from seed or transplant in sun or partial shade.

Chives (*Allium schoenoprasum*). Chives grow in clumps and look a bit like thin monkey grass. Onion chives have narrow leaves and lavender flowers; garlic chives (*A. tuberosum*) have white flowers. Plant in sun or partial shade.

Comfrey (*Symphytum officinale*). Known variously as "the healing herb," "knitbone," and "boneset," comfrey has large, fuzzy 10-inch-long leaves, spreads to 3 feet high by 3 feet or more wide, and has lovely bell-shaped pink or purple flowers which hang gracefully from vertical stems all summer. It grows in sun or shade, needs some water for best results, and should be used as an accent plant or in a large massing. Comfrey is evergreen during mild winters in the south. Even when it freezes to the ground, it returns each spring.

Dittany of Crete (*Origanum dictamnus*). This is an interesting herb for hanging baskets or patio containers, with small, soft, round gray leaves and small purple flowers summer through fall. Plant in full sun.

Elderberry (*Sambucus canadensis*). A large-growing, graceful shrubby perennial with edible purple-black berries from August through September, elderberry grows to 10 feet in most soils and has lovely white flower clusters in the summer. It is known to produce very fine, humus-laden soil and is a wonderful plant for attracting birds. It likes moist soil.

Garlic (*Allium sativum*). Besides warding off the "evil eye" and being the base for garlic tea, a natural disease fighter, and one of the world's healthiest and most delicious foods, garlic is also a good-looking landscape plant. Its foliage is dark green and grasslike. The flowers on some species are very interesting as they curve around and finally burst open in the early summer. It grows best in full sun but can take some shade. Elephant garlic— actually a leek—has large, decorative round flower balls.

Scented geraniums (*Pelargonium* spp.). These make excellent landscape plants because of their lovely foliage texture, wonderful fragrance, and delicate flowers. They are available in all sizes and many leaf shapes and textures, including deeply cut leaves and others that are soft and velvety. They are best used in pots or hanging baskets so they can be protected in the winter.

Ginkgo (*Ginkgo biloba*). Ginkgo is one of the oldest shade trees in the world. The leaves, used in food or tea, are reputed to be good for the memory. The tree has great, although short-lived, yellow fall color and an open, lacy overall effect.

Lamb's ear (*Stachys byzantina*). This tough, soft, fuzzy-leafed gray herb makes a good small-area groundcover that contrasts well with darker green plants. Lamb's ear grows in full sun or in fairly heavy shade. Its velvet-like foliage and lavender blossoms are delightful to see and to touch. The leaves make excellent natural bandages, and kids love them.

Lemon balm (*Melissa officinalis*). An easy-to-grow, fragrant herb with scalloped edge oval leaves, lemon balm has a lemony fragrance and is recommended for interplanting among vegetable and landscape plants to help repel pests and attract bees. Plant in sun or partial shade.

Lemongrass (*Cybopogon citratus*). This grasslike herb looks like a small-scale pampas grass. Its wonderful lemon scent makes it excellent for making tea. It rarely flowers, but the foliage has a lovely texture. If it freezes—which often happens in all but tropical areas—just plant new plants each year. It is best planted in full sun but can take some shade.

Lemon verbena (*Aloysia triphylla*). In addition to being one of the most delicious flavoring herbs, lemon verbena makes a wonderful addition to the landscape garden as well as the herb garden. It will freeze, so it's best treated as an annual. It can be used in a pot and brought indoors during the cold months. Plant in full sun.

Mint (*Mentha* spp.). Mints make good landscape groundcovers, but they all spread aggressively. *Mentha pulegium*, pennyroyal, is reported to repel fleas. Plant in sun or partial shade.

Mullein (*Verbascum thapsus*). Common mullein or old man's flannel is a big wildflower that looks like a large, upright version of lamb's ear. Its flowers are yellow, white, or purple depending on the variety. Mullein is a distinctive specimen plant to use in the landscape. Plant in full sun to partial shade.

Oregano (*Origanum* spp.). Oregano is used extensively in Greek and Italian food, and sometimes in Mexican dishes. It is excellent in sauces, soups, and salads. The strongest in flavor is Greek oregano, which is also an excellent cold-hardy ground-cover plant. Plant in sun or partial shade.

Perilla (*Perilla frutescens*). This easy-to-grow annual herb has dark burgundy leaves and growth habits similar to those of coleus and opal basil. Plant from seed or from transplants, and it will reseed aggressively each year. It makes a beautiful contrast with gray plants such as dusty miller wormwood or southern-wood. Plant in sun or partial shade.

Pineapple sage (*Salvia elegans*). An upright-growing herb with beautiful red flowers in the late summer or fall, pineapple sage perennializes through mild winters but should be used as an annual in most areas. It grows in sun or shade.

Purple coneflower (*Echinacea* spp.). This is an absolutely terrific perennial herb that should be used in every landscape. It blooms most of the summer with bright pink or white daisy-like flowers with yellow centers. It is drought tolerant and grows to over 3 feet in healthy soil. All parts of the plants are helpful to animals' immune systems—including our own.

Rosemary (*Rosmarinus officinalis*). Every garden should have at least one of these beautiful gray-green shrubs that can grow to a height of 4 feet. They freeze in hard winters but are certainly worth replanting every year if necessary. Rosemary has a nice texture, a marvelous pinelike fragrance, and beautiful light blue or white flowers. The low-growing groundcover type is *Rosmarinus prostratus*. Rosemary makes a great choice for pots and hanging baskets and is also an excellent bonsai plant.

Saffron (*Crocus sativus*). Saffron is an autumn-blooming crocus with purple flowers and long red stigmas from which the food flavor is made. Plant bulbs in the spring.

Sage (*Salvia officinalis*). Sage is a drought-tolerant evergreen perennial with grayish-green leaves. Several different selections are available, including variegated forms. Plant in sun or partial shade and be careful to avoid overwatering, since it can easily be drowned.

Salad burnet (*Poterium sanguisorba*). This compact, rosette-shaped evergreen herb reaches a height of 2 feet. Unimpressive flowers form on long stems growing out of the center of the plant. Its symmetrical shape and lacy foliage with a pleasant cucumber fragrance make it a good accent plant for sun or partial shade.

Southernwood (*Artemisia abrotanum*). Southernwood, my favorite artemisia, has finely textured dusty-gray foliage and a constant lemon scent that's stronger when the leaves are crushed. Plant in full sun in soil with excellent drainage.

Tansy (*Tanacetum vulgare*). This easy-to-grow ferny-leafed perennial herb blooms with button-like yellow flowers in the late summer to early fall. Chopped and crushed tansy leaves emit a very bitter taste and are an excellent repellent for ants. Plant in sun or shade, but preferably in sun.

Texas tarragon (*Tagetes lucida*). Unlike French tarragon, this excellent substitute is easy to grow. Its foliage has a strong fragrance, and it flowers with yellow blossoms in the late summer and early fall. Some people call it Mexican mint marigold.

Thyme (*Thymus vulgaris*). All thymes make excellent landscape plants. I especially like the creeping thymes, which make extremely fragrant groundcovers. Use between stepping stones, on borders, and in pockets in stone retaining walls. Plant in full sun for best results.

Wormwood (*Artemisia* spp.). Another tough gray-leaved plant that is extremely drought tolerant, wormwood is planted in full sun for texture and contrast with green plants.

Yarrow (*Achillea millifolium*). A beautiful plant year round, yarrow has lacy, fernlike foliage and is an evergreen perennial in warm climates. It has colorful flowers on tall stalks which bloom in the early summer and is available in white, pink, red, and purple.

Most herbs will do best in well-drained beds made of a mixture of compost and native soil. The best location is one with full sun in morning and at least some protection from the hot afternoon sun. It's amazing how strongly old-fashioned things like organics and herbs are returning to popularity. They are coming back simply because they work so well.

Organic Lawn Care

Organic lawn care is easy if you don't let a few weeds and different kinds of grasses bother you. Here are some guidelines on the most commonly used lawn grasses:

Bermudagrass is still the most popular grass of all because it is relatively easy to maintain as a green turf and is cheap to install. It grows only in full sun and can be a problem because of its aggressive habit of growing into planting beds while spreading by stolons and rhizomes. It looks fine growing mixed with St. Augustinegrass. Tex Turf 10 is the first step down in the selective hybridization of dwarf bermudas. The next step down to finer-textured bermudas is Tifway 419, then Tifgreen 328 and dwarf tiffs which are used on golf courses. Common bermudagrass is less susceptible to diseases and insects than the dwarf hybrids or St. Augustine. I still use bermuda some, but I prefer buffalograss in full-sun situations.

St. Augustinegrass is a wider-bladed grass than bermudagrass and can stand more shade—although it won't grow in heavy shade. It can freeze out in severe weather, even in the south. St. Augustinegrass decline is a problem disease in the common variety, but not in the hybrid cultivar 'Raleigh'. Because it requires more water and care than bermudagrass, it is farther down on my recommended list. It's a good choice for semi-shady areas in warm parts of the country, however.

Zoysia is an exotic-looking grass with thick, succulent dark green foliage. The only problem with zoysia, other than that it won't grow in shade, is that it is so slow growing. I would never use it in an area that gets much foot traffic from people or pets.

A dog or the mail carrier walking the same path regularly will kill it out. For a beautiful grass to look at and not use too much, however, 'Meyer' zoysia is hard to beat. The other varieties, such as 'Emerald', aren't as good.

Buffalograss is the best choice for lawns in full sun. It has a soft, beautiful appearance and requires little water and even less fertilization. Some people have tried hard to convince us that the flowers of the male plants are ugly, but the wispy white flags which are often misidentified as seeds are actually quite attractive. If you are hung up on their appearance, sterile female hybrid choices such as 'Prairie' are available. They are good but expensive. Whether you buy native or hybrid buffalograss, you'll be pleased with the results.

Cool-season grasses include bentgrass, bluegrass, ryegrass, fescue, and other more northern-adapted grasses. These grasses are used as permanent grasses in cool or cold climates. Some are used for overseeding the warm-season grasses in the south, and they are also sometimes used in shady areas in warm climates. Cool-season grasses are of the bunch type rather than spreading like bermuda and buffalo. All grasses are maintained in basically the same way except that bunch grasses should be mowed higher than spreading grasses.

The difference in organic and chemical lawn care is considerable. The latter involves ignoring nature's systems and force-feeding the plants with high-nitrogen, highly water soluble synthetic fertilizers and spraying chemical pesticides on the insect and disease outbreaks that are directly related to the poor fertilization program. The organic method, on the other hand, looks at the soil to determine its condition and then adjusts the balance of chemistry, biology, and physics. The organic gardener or lawn-care professional feeds the soil and lets the soil feed the plants.

The watering schedule is critical to organic lawn care. The most common mistake is watering too often and not deep enough at each watering. The result is weak, shallow root systems and the wasteful use of too much water. Watering less often and deeper each time prevents salt buildup, limits waste from evaporation, and encourages larger, healthier root systems. Putting down about 1 inch at each watering is a good basic starting point. As with nature, organic programs are dynamic and need to be adjusted from time to time.

An organic program will give you not only a beautiful lawn but a comfortable place where your pets and children can play safely.

As I have already emphasized, if you mow your own lawn, you should stop spending the money, time, and energy required to bag the grass clippings. *Don't bag 'em!*

There are several reasons why the grass clippings should be left on the lawn, and there are even stronger arguments for not putting clippings in plastic bags and leaving them on the street curb for the garbage collectors to pick up and haul to the dump. Clippings provide the critical organic material that the beneficial microorganisms need to create natural fertilizer. In addition, grass clippings contain nutrients, and a large percentage of those nutrients accumulate in the leaf tips. University studies have shown that nitrogen in grass clippings left on the lawn can be back in the living grass plants in less than two weeks.

Many cities in this country have a serious problem with the amount of available land left for landfills and garbage dumps. As much as 40 percent of landfill volume is attributed to grass clippings, leaves, and tree chips. Grass makes up the greatest percentage of all the vegetative materials, and the plastic bags are another serious environmental concern.

The fact that this problem even exists is ridiculous because the clippings are beneficial to turf and should be left on the ground. Some experts say that the mowing frequency needs to be increased to once every five days instead of once a week, but I don't agree. If organic fertilizers are used, the grass will be healthy and green but slower growing.

An extra mowing may sometimes be needed after a rain because of the extra nitrogen and oxygen that is produced in a thunderstorm.

Any time excess grass clippings accumulate, put them in the compost pile, not in garbage bags. If you own a quality mulching mower, you never have to worry about excess clippings because they are ground into a fine powder and don't accumulate on the surface.

To anticipate an often-asked question, no, leaving the clippings on the lawn does not cause thatch buildup. Just the opposite, in fact—the clippings, along with organic fertilizers, provide food for the microorganisms and fertilizer nutrients for the grass. Chemical fertilizers and pesticides kill the microorganisms, causing the thatch to remain and become a problem.

Fall: The Best Time to Garden

Fall is the best time of the year for many gardening activities. First of all, it's simply the most pleasant time to work in the garden. Crisp, clear skies and mild temperatures are a treat in themselves. In addition, it's the time to prepare, plant, and pile up the compost. If you were going to wait for spring, it may surprise you to learn that spring is one of the worst times to prepare beds and plant new materials. Spring is the time for the most active top growth, but fall is the most active time for root growth.

Plant roots put on a strong spurt of growth in the fall and continue to grow all winter. Then, when spring arrives, plants will have large, aggressive root systems, large, long-lasting blooms, lush new growth, and more hardiness than you have ever experienced with a chemical program. When summer arrives, your plants will have much stronger heat and drought tolerance, and when winter rolls around, their increased cold-hardiness will be evident. Organically healthy soil has more life, more energy and more heat—and therefore protects plant roots from freeze damage. Chemically treated soil does not have this advantage.

Soil is the key to plant health. Soil is a whole system of living organisms, minerals, water, and air. It's a dynamic community of interacting relationships which are in a constant state of growth, adjustment, and change. What's most fascinating is that soil will improve itself if you simply stop hurting it. As it improves itself, it will become softer and more aerated and will drain better. It will also hold just the right amount of water for a long period of time.

If the soil is alive and healthy, it is rich in humus, balanced in minerals, and active with microscopic plants and animals. The energy and nutrition produced in the soil will be transferred to the plants, and they in turn will have a very powerful natural resistance to insect pests and diseases. If you establish the right conditions—no pesticides, no synthetic fertilizer, and proper watering techniques—nature will balance the soil for you in the same way that it balances it in the forest. However, it is possible to speed up the natural process.

If you haven't already begun an organic program, fall is an excellent time to start, because the soil and the root systems of plants will improve all through the winter.

Here are some guidelines for beginning your organic program The Natural Way. If you start using these techniques and products this fall, not only will you soon be hooked, but by this time next year you will wonder why everyone in the world isn't using organics.

Raise your mower height to at least 2½ inches and leave the clippings on the ground. Mechanically aerate all lawn areas. Fertilize with a 100 percent organic fertilizer at 20 pounds per 1,000 square feet, and mulch all bare soil in the planting beds with at least 4 inches of shredded hardwood bark or native wood chips. Spray all planting areas and lawns with a mixture of fish emulsion, seaweed, and molasses. Mulch the ground surface of all newly planted trees and if necessary (i.e., if you have been listening to the wrong people), take the staking and wrapping off the tree.

Perennials that bloom in the spring should be planted right away. Established stands of spring- or summer-blooming perennials that have been in one spot for four or five years should be divided carefully, spread out, and moved to new locations. This thinning of perennial stands rejuvenates their foliage growth, root development, and flower production. Fall-blooming plants should be enjoyed now and moved in the spring. The easy rule of thumb to remember is *divide and move perennials in the season opposite their bloom time.* In either case, be sure to water thoroughly and mulch the bare soil after the transplanting is done.

Fall is the time to plant wildflowers, if you didn't do it in late summer. Use a native mix—no exotic introduced species—and treat the seed with one of the commercial biostimulators or with natural vinegar. Make sure bare soil is exposed by lightly tilling the grass and weeds to a depth of about 1 inch. The key is to make sure that the seeds are planted *in* the soil, not just broadcast on the surface and left to parch in the sun. Raking the seed lightly into the soil will make a great difference in the germination of the seed and the success of the wildflower stand in the spring.

It's also time to start the compost pile if you haven't already done so. All vegetative matter from the garden and landscape should be either left on the ground as mulch or put into the compost pile. All of the waste in the landscape garden should go into the compost pile. Put in everything—dead tree limbs, sawdust, weeds, dead plants, animal manure, animal hair, dust, excess lawn clippings, leaves, twigs, and nongreasy kitchen scraps. Chop up the large pieces, and wet the material as it's added to the pile. Pile it all up on the ground or on a concrete area if you have room. If space is limited, use a container made of hay bales or wire mesh. The store-bought containers are okay but expensive, and their capacity is modest. Turn the material at least monthly by dumping it out and re-piling—the more often it is turned, the speedier the process.

Leave the grass as high as you can during the transition to cooler weather, and apply a 100 percent organic fertilizer if your soil is not yet healthy. You can tell by looking and feeling whether the soil is chemically, biologically, and physically balanced. Good soil, no matter what its color, will be soft, crumbly, and full of earthworms.

Fall is an excellent time to begin the organic program, if you haven't already, because the soil and the root system of plants will improve all through the winter.

Low-Maintenance Landscape Design

A house or an office building looks its best the day it is finished; landscape gardens should not only look good immediately after they are completed, but get better every year.

Poorly designed gardens can be pleasing to most people if they are maintained well, while well-designed gardens which are poorly maintained are usually failures. Therefore, the design of any garden, large or small, should include maintenance considerations in the early planning stages. Gardens are designed every day that look great on paper, look good when planted, but look terrible two years later. That can be avoided by designing gardens that are easy to maintain.

Landscaping, unlike architecture, is never static. Gardens contain structures and living organisms that change seasonally and continue to mature each year. The metamorphic change that takes place between the date of installation and the later years is quite significant. Most gardens have at least two lives, the first mostly in full sun as the newly planted trees are maturing, the second beginning as the trees grow and shade the ground to create a completely different environment. It's very important to understand from the beginning that gardens change and that change, if planned for carefully, can insure the yearly improvement of your home or business environment.

Maintenance is directly related to the soil preparation, the selection of plant materials, and the quality of installation methods. Bed preparation should produce live, organic soil that is rich in humus and rock minerals. Successful plant-material selection means choosing plants that will not only live, but thrive and grow vigorously with a minimum of maintenance. When plant materials are not happy about where they are placed, the resulting maintenance will increase proportionally.

Generally, the larger plants (trees and large shrubs) need the least amount of soil amendments and bed preparation; the smaller plants (small shrubs, groundcovers, annuals, and perennials) need the most. The theory is to change the soil around new plants only if the entire root zone can be improved. The larger plants, whose root systems will eventually grow out beyond any prepared bed, should be planted in the existing native soil. These plants should be allowed to acclimate to the native soil as soon as possible.

Drainage is a key piece of the puzzle. Plants can't be healthy in wet, poorly drained soil; they need oxygen for healthy root growth. Even if the correct plants have been selected, they will fail if the soil does not drain. Avoiding flat and low spots is therefore of critical importance. An underground drainage system of PVC pipe set in gravel is sometimes needed in hard-to-drain areas. Organic soil amendments, natural fertilizers, and good horticultural techniques will also improve drainage.

I feel very strongly that grass should be planted in the native soil, with no foreign soil added, since the addition of such amendments as sandy loam on top of clay soils can cause problems. Solid rock on the surface of the ground is the only exception, and even then native topsoil, rather than soil that is foreign to the area, should be used to cover the rock.

Give plant materials a healthy, natural start, and in return they will be much easier to maintain and will provide the atmosphere and beauty you desire.

6 Food Crops

Starting Seeds Organically

To start your organic garden from scratch, it's best to begin with organically grown seed that is open pollinated (i.e., non-hybrids, or species that can be grown again from the seed of your own crop). There are many good sources, including Seeds of Change, P.O. Box 280, Gila, NM 88038, Shepherd's Garden Seeds, Shipping Office, 30 Irene Street, Torrington, CT 06790, and Southern Exposure Seed Exchange, P.O. Box 158, North Garden, VA 22959. Other good-quality seeds are available, but try to avoid seed that has been treated with chemical pesticides. Many hybrid seeds have been engineered to work best with high-nitrogen synthetic fertilizers and pesticides; you'll find that those don't perform so well in an organic program.

The planting soil for starting seed should be the next consideration. Finely textured potting soils are best, especially when growing plants with tiny seed. Your potting soil should be alive. Living potting soils contain compost, earthworm castings, and other living soil amendments. If you use a sterile, commercially made potting soil such as Jiffy, Peters, or Metro Mix, add a generous proportion of earthworm castings or compost to the mix— as much as one-third of the volume. Homemade potting soil can be made by mixing 4 parts compost (homemade or store bought), 3 parts sand (lava sand is best), 2 parts earthworm castings, and 1 part colloidal phosphate. Again, try to buy ingredients that are finely screened and intended specifically for use in seed starting.

Planting pots and trays can vary tremendously. Local nurseries and seed catalogs usually have a good selection; from them you can obtain plastic pots, plastic trays with plastic covers, and Styrofoam pots, some of which are to be watered from above, others to be watered from below. Peat pots (individual pots made of a peat-moss material) are also available, as are peat pellets, which look like flat biscuits when dry, but grow in height when watered. I like to use soil blocks made from homemade potting soil. Soil-block molds are used to make these blocks, and no containers are necessary. The soil-block mold forms the planting medium into free-standing soil squares, and the seed can be planted directly into the squares. These blocks provide excellent drainage, can be planted directly into the soil once the plant has established roots, and are a very good way to start seeds The Natural Way. Another good method is to fill old egg cartons or ice-cube trays with potting soil after punching a hole in the bottom of each compartment. These work very well and are a good way to recycle otherwise discardable products.

To determine when to plant the seed, it's best to follow the instructions on the seed packet, which will usually explain when to plant in relation to the average last-freeze date in your area.

The soil should be fertilized at the time of planting with a soaking of a 1–2 percent solution of fish emulsion and liquid seaweed. The seed should be misted prior to planting with a 5 percent solution of the same mix or a biostimulant such as Agrispon, Medina, or Roots. If a high-quality, fine-textured compost such as earthworm castings has been added to the potting soil, the only additional fertilization needed prior to the plants' being set out in the garden would be a weekly misting of the same organic liquid products. Alfalfa tea (made from 1 cup of alfalfa meal in 5 gallons of water) is another excellent liquid material to use early in the propagation process.

Be sure to keep the seed flats in a moderately warm, brightly lit place so the small plants won't grow tall and spindly. If natural light from windows, skylights, or greenhouses is not available, bright artificial light is needed. When the transplants have several leaves, they can be moved to an outside location protected from late freezes. Cold frames are excellent for this purpose. When the temperature outside is right for the crop you've started, plant the seedlings in raised rows, hills, or beds and mulch around the small plants to cover all bare soil.

In order to take advantage of the benefit of using heirloom or open-pollinated plants, it is important to understand how to save some seed for next year's crops. Open-pollinated plants will come back true from seed, whereas hybrids will not and have to be repurchased every year.

While the current crop is in production, mark the best plants with paper tags or twist ties so they'll be easy to find when in fruit. Save a high-quality fruit, tomato, pepper, or whatever. Using one that a bird has pecked is okay—in fact it may be a good sign—birds have excellent taste.

Cut the fruit open, and clean the seeds thoroughly in a big kitchen strainer to prevent them from growing mold. Spread the seeds to dry on several thicknesses of newspaper in a dim, cool place. When they are dry, store them in clean glass containers in the refrigerator. Add a small amount of diatomaceous earth to remove any trace of moisture. Don't be dopey like me and think you can remember what's in each container. I've learned the hard way to label each container with the date and variety. You will now be ready when it's time to plant the next season's crop. Alternatively, you can leave it to the professionals and buy new seed each year—the choice is yours. I usually do a little of both.

Garlic: King of Vegetables, Herbs, and Spices

Everyone who has a plot of ground or a pot should grow garlic. This plant has more varied uses and more significant benefits than probably any other plant on earth. Garlic (*Allium sativum*) is one of the most nutritious and health-giving foods available, but it also offers many other benefits.

One of the most pleasant facts about garlic is that it is easy to grow. The cloves should be planted in a similar way to onions, 3–4 inches apart and 1½–2 inches deep. Garlic is shallow rooted and is greatly helped by mulching, as are most plants. It is not a high water user and is tolerant of relatively wet or dry soils, although less watering close to maturity is important for the proper development of the bulbs. Cool weather is important for garlic. Since temperatures between 32° and 50° F. for thirty days are necessary for proper bulb development, it's best to plant in the fall. For larger bulbs, cut the flower stalk off as soon as it starts to emerge.

When the tops begin to dry and fall over in July or August, the bulbs are ready for harvest. Don't wait until the entire top is brown. When the foliage first starts to turn, dig the garlic out gently with a turning fork. You can cut the tops off or tie or braid them and hang them in the garage or a partially shaded place where they can dry. They will store well in a cool, dry area for a long time. Use your garlic freely, but save some of the larger bulbs for the next year's planting. If you already have some growing, that's great; if not, you can buy some from grocery stores or the farmer's market. Try to buy organically grown garlic because it will be healthier to eat and will have greater pest-control powers.

Garlic is great for eating and for seasoning various foods. There is strong evidence that garlic eaten regularly can lower blood pressure, and it tastes great on many foods. Try garlic powder on almost any meat dish. Fresh garlic is even better. Don't shy away from this great herb because of "garlic breath." Chew on a few fresh leaves of parsley or sweet basil; the high chlorophyll content of these herbs will neutralize the garlic smell. Of course, if everyone eats garlic, no one will notice the smell.

Garlic has lots of other uses besides culinary ones. Here are a few of them:

Mosquito control. When poured or sprayed into standing water, stagnant ponds, and other wet breeding spots, garlic oil will control mosquito larvae quite well. Since spraying the air is one of the most polluting and least effective methods of trying to control mosquitoes, it would be wise to try this completely non-toxic control right away.

General insect control. For years organic gardeners have used garlic tea to control aphids, spider mites, whiteflies, and other garden pests. Garlic grown in a circle around a fruit tree is said to be a good repellent of fruit-tree borers. It can be inter-planted among ornamental landscape plants as well as food crops to ward off various pests. Herbalists say that roses are given a substantial amount of protection by garlic planted nearby, and tomatoes seldom have red-spider problems when garlic is planted nearby. Be careful, though—garlic will slow the growth of beans and peas. Why does it discriminate? I don't know.

Garlic tea sprayed on plant foliage before heavy insect infestations occur works as a powerful repellent to most problem insects. One of my organic friends pours garlic tea on fire-ant mounds, and he claims excellent results. When hot-pepper oil is added to the garlic, it becomes a mild but effective insecticide.

Fungicidal control. Herbalists have used garlic and pepper tea for years to control insect pests, and those with the most experience claim that it also has very real fungicidal powers. Garlic will aid significantly in the control of powdery mildew, downy mildew, rust, tomato blight, and other disease problems.

Even such scientists as Charles L. Wilson of the U.S. Department of Agriculture are now saying that members of the garlic and pepper families have effective fungicidal components. They are currently researching how those properties can be used on a commercial basis. I'd probably recommend just making a bigger batch of the same stuff we've been using all along.

Rodent repellent. Rabbits and other unwanted visitors to the garden can sometimes be repelled by the smell of garlic spray on the vegetables and ornamental plants. Garlic spray on trash cans can help keep raccoons and cats away. Dry hot-pepper powder (cayenne or habanero) is sometimes needed for stubborn animals. These techniques work fairly well for deer problems.

Many recipes exist for garlic tea. Here are a few that I find effective:

1. Put two large garlic bulbs in a blender with water and liquefy. Strain the solids off by using cheesecloth or a fine strainer and add the soupy liquid to a gallon of water. This concentrate can be used at the rate of 2 tablespoons to ¼ cup of concentrate per gallon. Spray any and all plants as often as you feel the need.

2. The same as above, but add 2 jalapeño, habanero, or cayenne peppers to the mixture when blending. This blend is the basic garlic/pepper tea.

3. The same as garlic/pepper tea above, but add 2 tablespoons of mineral oil to the concentrate. This blend is used for hard-to-control pests.

Does garlic really keep the vampires away? Maybe—there are none around my house.

Organic Tomatoes

The nation's greatest pastime is gardening—and the gardener's favorite crop is tomatoes. If you prefer the taste of a homegrown tomato to that of store-bought ones, just wait until you taste a homegrown *organic* tomato. Growing tomatoes in healthy, living soil without artificial fertilizers and pesticides produces not only better taste but higher and more balanced food nutrition as well.

Just as with organic landscaping, it all starts with the soil. There are several good ways to build organic beds for growing tomatoes, but they all have the same basic ingredients; native soil, lots of compost, natural rock minerals, plenty of oxygen, and excellent drainage.

The best time to plant tomatoes is the day after the last freeze—if anyone can guess when that is. Most folks go ahead and plant with the hope that freezing weather is over. A wise approach I learned some years ago is to grow tomatoes from seed and set out small plants in early spring but save a duplicate supply of plants to use as replacements should a late freeze hit— as it often does! Tomatoes should be planted 24–36 inches apart in full sun.

To speed up your early production of tomatoes, try this technique. Move plants from 2-inch pots into 4-inch pots, leave the plants outside during mild weather, and move them inside when the temperature falls. This allows the root system and the foliage to develop during the early spring when it's too early to set the plants out in the garden. The plants in 4-inch pots, when rootbound, can be moved up to 1-gallon containers if time allows. The increased size of the root system is the great benefit of this technique. Earlier tomato production will result.

The ultimate planting site for tomatoes can be a container, especially if you have limited garden space. Large clay pots or wooden whiskey or pickle barrels work well if they have drainage holes in the bottom. Be sure to clean wooden barrels thoroughly with a nonphosphate soap, vinegar, or hydrogen peroxide. The potting soil both for this ultimate large container and for the small containers mentioned above should be "organic." Isn't all potting soil organic? you ask. No, not unless it's alive. Typical potting soil contains basically inert or dead materials, such as peat moss, perlite, vermiculite, and sand. Those ingredients are fine if the mixture also contains living compost. If the term "sterile" or "pasteurized" appears on your bag of a ready-to-use potting soil, it can be brought to life by adding a good-quality compost and/or earthworm castings. The best potting soils on the market contain compost, earthworm castings, rock minerals, and other organic ingredients. A good potting soil mix that can be made at home is as follows:

4 parts compost (homemade or store bought)
3 parts sand (lava sand is best)
2 parts earthworm castings
1 part colloidal phosphate
Organic fertilizer, at 2 teaspoons per gallon, 4 ounces per cubic
    foot, or 7 pounds per cubic yard

In the garden, the same living soil is needed. In fact, tomatoes are heavy feeders and do best when extra amounts of humus are available. Earthworm castings and high-quality compost that is at least 20 percent manure are the best sources of humus and natural nutrients. Unlike many vegetables, tomatoes actually prefer to be planted in the same place year after year. Raise the planting area by building flat-topped hills or rows and furrows. The raised beds created by either technique improves drainage and soil aeration. Oxygen is very important to the health of the root system.

A unique planting device is the Japanese planting ring. The ring can be made of welded wire, chicken wire, hog wire, or concrete-reinforcing wire. Some people even use wooden barrels with no bottoms. The ring, which should be placed on well-prepared raised soil, should be 3–4 feet tall and filled with compost and/or raw compost ingredients such as manure and leaves. The diameter of the ring can range from 2 to 7 feet. The tomato plants should be planted on the outside of the ring, approximately 24 inches apart. They can be staked, wired to the ring, or have their own individual wire cages. They are irrigated by watering the compost. The water traveling through the compost carries natural fertilizer to the tomato plants at each watering. The leachate from the compost is loaded with a wonderful blend of natural nutrients.

In a more traditional garden planting, tomatoes should be fertilized with natural fertilizers such as earthworm castings, composted manure, or cottonseed meal every two to three weeks.

When setting out transplants, toss a small handful of colloidal phosphate and earthworm castings into the hole, and plant tomatoes deep because they have the ability to sprout roots from the stem, which will make the plant more stable. Cut or tear roots that are pot bound.

Organic disease and pest control will be quite easy if you followed the bed-preparation instructions. Diseases for the most part are controlled by the balanced soil and specifically by the healthy population of beneficial microorganisms. The energy created in healthy soil is transmitted into the plants, and natural pest resistance is established. During rare outbreaks of disease or insect attack, organic pesticides can be used. Diseases can be controlled with baking-soda spray (1 rounded tablespoon per gallon of water), natural vinegar spray (1½ ounces per gallon of water), or copper or sulfur sprays. Insects can be controlled with garlic/pepper tea and seaweed for aphids and spider mites and Bt (*Bacillus thuringiensis*) for caterpillars. If you want more horsepower, pyrethrum, rotenone, or sabadilla can be used, but this usually isn't necessary. A foliar spray of liquid seaweed and fish emulsion every 1 to 2 weeks will help control most pests and feed the plants at the same time. Water regularly to maintain an even moisture level and, as always, mulch bare soil under the plants with coarse-textured organic matter. Bare soil should never be exposed under tomatoes.

The Natural Way to Grow Pecans

Yes, you can maintain pecan trees organically. No, you don't need to spray the trees twelve times a year, nor do you necessarily need to spray zinc on the trees every year. Here's The Natural Way to grow pecans.

Prepare the soil by aerating, tilling, or ripping to get more oxygen in the ground. Spray the soil with Agrispon, Medina, Bioform or other bio-stimulant. Make sure the planting area drains well.

If you have an orchard, plant the trees at least 40 feet apart; 60 feet is better. If the trees are for your home garden, plant them as close together as you like.

Plant a mix of varieties. Check with your local extension service or nursery for the recommended varieties for your area. I like to include at least a few native pecans along with the hybrids if there's room, since they are more pest resistant and the nuts have excellent taste, even though they are smaller and tougher than the hybrids.

Plant the trees in rough-sided, wide holes, backfill with the native soil from the hole, settle the soil with water, cover the planting-hole area with a 1-inch layer of compost, and cover the compost with 4 inches of shredded hardwood bark, wood chips, or hay.

Settle the soil around the roots with water. Don't add peat moss, foreign soil, or fertilizer to the backfill, and don't tamp the soil, wrap the trunk, stake the tree, or cut back the top.

If you don't use a thick mulch layer under the trees and don't have landscape plants, plant a green-manure cover crop of hairy vetch, at 25 pounds per acre, and cereal rye grain (elbon) or oats, at 25 pounds per acre. In your home garden, use a much higher rate. If bare soil still exists in any areas in the spring, plant black-eyed peas or buckwheat as a summer cover crop. If the trees are being planted in a lawn area, don't plant cover crops but do maintain the mulch above the root ball as long as possible.

Feed pecan trees by one of these three methods:

1. Broadcast a 100 percent organic fertilizer to the root zone at 20 pounds per 1,000 square feet.
2. Broadcast manure at 2–5 tons per acre.
3. Broadcast compost at 2–5 tons per acre.

The long-term fertilization requirements should be based on a soil test from a lab that gives organic recommendations. Two I know of are Texas Plant and Soil Lab, Rt. 7, Box 213Y, Edinburg, TX 78539 (210/383-0739), and Timberleaf, 5569 State Street, Albany, OH 45710 (614/698-3681). In the beginning, two applications of fertilizer (in spring and fall) are usually needed, but as the soil health improves, less fertilizer will be needed. Only one application a year is needed after the soil balance has been improved.

For additional nut production, spray the foliage with a mixture of fish emulsion, seaweed, molasses, and vinegar. Add a biostimulant if your budget allows. A monthly application is ideal but not essential. Foliar sprays have the greatest effect if done early in the morning or around dusk. Zinc or other micro-nutrients should be added to the mix only if the soil test shows a deficiency in those specific mineral elements.

Beneficial insects provide the best pest-control program. Starting in early spring, release a succession of ladybugs, green lacewings, and trichogramma wasps. A good schedule is as follows:

April. Release ladybugs, at 1,500–2,000 per 1,000 square feet, or trichogramma wasps, at 20,000 eggs per acre, weekly.

May. Release green lacewings, at 2,000–4,000 eggs per acre, every two weeks.

June. Release green lacewings, at 2,000 eggs per acre, every two weeks.

August. Release green lacewings, at 2,000 eggs per acre, every two weeks.

September. Release green lacewings, at 2,000 eggs per acre, every two weeks.

The rate per acre works for residential lots, but it can be doubled to speed up the process. If pesticides are not being used, beneficial insects will naturalize, and the number of releases can be greatly reduced each year.

Aphids, weevils, and pecan-nut casebearers are the most common pecan pests, but they are easily controlled with beneficial bugs. Occasional heavy infestations of aphids can be eliminated with a strong water spray. Most fungus and disease problems will be kept in check with healthy soil, but occasional infestations can be controlled with baking-soda or vinegar spray (4 teaspoons baking soda and 1 teaspoon soap in 1 gallon of water or 1½ ounces of apple cider vinegar per gallon of water). Garlic tea sprayed as a preventative will help control most insect and disease pests and will not hurt the beneficial insects. Use 2 tablespoons of a concentrate per gallon. Check the label on commercial products.

Birds are also an important part of the pest-control program, so don't forget to feed them.

Switching to Organic Fruit

Each year I get hundreds of questions about organics. Here's a typical example from a potential convert:

Dear Howard:
I have a small orchard of peaches, pears, plums, apples, and pecans. For the third year I have been following the recommended chemical spray schedule from the extension service using the proper fungicides and insecticides. My fruit again this year is covered with fungal spots and brown rot. Plus, the fruit is very small even though I have thinned the fruit as recommended by the experts. I'm ready to try something else. One more thing I should mention is that I regularly use Round Up under the trees to eliminate the weeds. Could that be part of my problem?
    N. L., Dallas.

Here's how I answered:

It's tempting to say "see—I told you the chemical approach doesn't work," but of course I won't do that. I will point out that your biggest problem is bare, unhealthy soil. The chemical spray schedule not only doesn't work, it makes the problem worse. It's critical to have a living mulch of cover crops or a blanket of organic mulch under the trees. It's impossible for the soil to be healthy without a forest floor type covering of mulch or green manure crop. If the soil is healthy, disease problems are few to none. To get on the right track, send some soil to a testing lab and ask for some organic recommendations. When the test results come back, look at the base saturation of calcium and magnesium. If the calcium is more than 80 percent, add sulfur to the soil at 5 pounds per 1,000 square feet. If calcium is less than 60 percent, add high-calcium lime to the soil at 20–40 pounds per 1,000 square feet. If you don't want to fool with all that, just add 4 inches of compost and cottonseed meal or another fertilizer at

20 pounds per 1,000 square feet. Apply your 100 percent organic fertilizer at least twice a year. Spring and early summer works well but some gardeners like spring and fall better. Both work.

Drop the poison sprays and start spraying every month, or if the budget and time allows, every two weeks with fish emulsion and seaweed. Spraying the foliage is primary but include the limbs, the trunks, and the ground. For added help, add 1 tablespoon of apple cider or other natural vinegar and 1 tablespoon blackstrap molasses to each gallon of spray. If the soil test shows that magnesium is deficient, add 1 tablespoon of Epsom salts to the mix. These ingredients can provide minerals that aren't available from the soil.

Back to the Round Up question—that's how I knew you had bare soil and no mulch. To help you decide whether or not to use chemical herbicides in the future, read what Dr. Carl Whitcomb says on pages 379 through 381 in his book *Establishment and Maintenance of Landscape Plants.* His experiments have shown that this product can injure plants through the soil and roots. If a thick mulch blanket is kept on the ground under the trees, there will be no need for chemical herbicides because there won't be any weeds.

Herb Tea

Herbs are used for cooking, medication, fragrance, and landscaping. Among the best food flavoring herbs are rosemary, Texas tarragon, savory, basil, lemongrass, thyme, and oregano. Many herbs have excellent medicinal uses. Aloe vera is the world's best natural burn treatment, and comfrey juice will quickly ease the pain of insect stings. Garlic, ginger, purple coneflower, and ginkgo are even accepted by the conventional medical community for their great health-improving powers. Herbs also make wonderful landscape plants for ornamental beds or pots. Some of my favorites are bay (best to put in pots and bring indoors in winter), oregano, and thyme for groundcover. Many are used for their colorful flowers—salvia, elderberry, Texas tarragon, and tansy, for example. Many herbs, such as comfrey, mullein, and lamb's ear, are used for their dramatic foliage. Some herbs are excellent landscape trees. Among the best are redbud, ginkgo, sassafras, and linden.

But there's another use for herbs: making tea. I love to drink herb tea. It's good anytime but especially in the evening, particularly at bedtime. My family has been into drinking herb tea for some time—in fact it has become a year-round ritual. Some of our favorite ingredients are lemon verbena, peppermint (especially chocolate peppermint), lemon balm, lemongrass, rosemary, ginkgo, purple coneflower, lavender, thyme, spearmint, and camomile. Hot tea is good at night in hot and cold weather. Herb teas are relaxing, many will help you breathe easier, and some will help you sleep better.

To prepare herb teas, simply pick fresh leaves from herbs, put them in a teapot, and pour slightly cooled boiling water over them. Don't boil the leaves. I normally use ½ cup of fresh leaves or a tablespoon of dried leaves. The color is usually a light yellow/green. Let the brew steep for three to ten minutes depending on your taste, and then enjoy a nice cup of hot tea. Some people like to let the tea leaves remain in the water longer. If the steeping time is overdone, tannic acid will be released into the tea, making it bitter. A single herb or a mix of various plants can be used. I often use chocolate peppermint as a base and add various other herbs to create a different taste each night. For a nice lemony tea, try a blend of lemongrass (my favorite lemon-flavored herb), lemon verbena, and lemon balm.

These natural teas are great with nothing added, but lemon juice or honey can be added for taste. Texas herbalist Odena Brennam helped me get on the air to do my radio show one morning despite a sore throat and headache the night before with the following recipe: chocolate peppermint, a squeeze of lemon juice, and honey. I once got sinus headaches whenever the weather made a big change. Not any more, thanks to that recipe. By the way, it also helps if you use clean, filtered water.

Chlorine and other contaminants can ruin the taste of any good drink.

After you have finished drinking the tea, what you have left over in the teapot has a couple of uses. Even if it has honey, it makes a good organic fertilizer. Just pour it on the plants after it has cooled. Of course, don't overdo it; too much watering is hard on plants. It could also be put into your foliar spray solution. The other use is to drink it cold over ice the next day. Toss a couple of fresh leaves into your iced drink for additional flavor. Don't forget to pick a good supply of leaves, flowers, and such to dry and store for wintertime use. You can also plan to grow some of these wonderful plants in pots indoors this winter.

7 Wildlife

Bats

People's response to bats is usually similar to or worse than their response to the sight of a rat or a cockroach. It would be hard to find much very praiseworthy to write about the latter pair, but there's plenty to praise about bats.

First, let me briefly try to dispel the falsehoods about bats. Most bats don't suck blood from the necks of beautiful women—or ugly men, for that matter; in fact, the only blood-loving bats are the vampire bats, and they live in Latin America. Some bats eat the nectar from flowers, and others eat flying insects. Bats aren't ugly—well not too ugly; they are quite interesting-looking furry mammals with large wings. They do look somewhat peculiar hanging upside down in caves and under bridges, but their mysterious sleeping habits shouldn't bother anyone, especially since they do all of their beneficial work at night and don't bother anybody during the day.

Bats are intelligent, friendly, gentle, clean, and little if any health threat. They spread less rabies than do cats and dogs. In fact, according to bat expert Merlin Tuttle, more people die from dog attacks annually than have died throughout history from contact with bats. Because of the misunderstanding of this wonderfully helpful creature, its population is dwindling all over the world.

What do bats do that's so helpful? The nectar-eating bats aid the pollination of food crops, primarily tropical fruits in warm regions but also the agave from which tequila is made. The insect-eating bats rid the night skies of huge amounts of mosquitoes and other flying insects.

In Texas, which has the highest population density of bats in the United States, there are two particularly interesting bat communities. One is the largest urban colony, which is estimated at close to a million bats roosting under the Congress Avenue bridge in downtown Austin. The other, located in Bracken Cave, a natural cave north of San Antonio, has been proclaimed by *National Geographic* to be the largest concentration of mammals in a single place on earth. If the one million bats in Austin eat an estimated twenty thousand pounds of mosquitoes each night, imagine the benefit we receive from the twenty million bats that leave Bracken Cave every night from April to October to feed on insects!

You've probably already figured out the point of all this. One of nature's best natural fertilizers is—you got it!—bat guano. Bat guano contains from 1 to 10 percent nitrogen and many trace elements. The analysis will vary with the age of the guano, but it is usually rich in nitrogen because it is protected in the caves from the rain, so the nutrients are not leached away. It has natural fungicidal qualities, little chance of being contaminated with pesticides or chemicals, and little odor compared with other animal manures. It is an excellent supplemental fertilizer for flowers and a standard item on organic landscape specifications for use on all flowering plants.

Look into the sky at dusk, and you will often see four friends you should be thankful for: the nighthawk, the chimney swift, the barn swallow, and the bat. The bat is the one with the quick, darting moves and the clicking sound.

Bat houses should be positioned at least 10 to 15 feet or more above the ground, facing east or southeast to catch the morning sun. The entry should be free of obstructions such as branches or structures.

If you are interested in receiving more information about our furry flying friends, write or call Bat Conservation International, P.O. Box 162603, Austin, TX 78716 (512/327-9721).

Attracting Hummingbirds and Butterflies

Hummingbirds and butterflies are easy to attract, especially if you are organic. One sure way to *limit* their presence is to spray chemical pesticides on a regular basis.

Hummingbird feeders are helpful in attracting these beautiful little birds in the summer. Clear sugar water is all that is needed if the feeder has red tips on the tubes or other red color on the feeder. To make the sugar solution, add one part of sugar to three or four parts of water. It is important to change the sugar solution every day or two so the solution doesn't spoil and cause disease. The birds won't be present until spring, but fall is the ideal time of year to plant red blooming vines and flowers such as coral honeysuckle, autumn sage, Turk's cap, red columbine, and Indian paintbrush. For best results, use plants that have long, tubular flowers. Other good choices include anisacanthus, pomegranate, red yucca, trumpet vine, and dwarf powderpuff.

Butterflies are attracted to various colors. Some of the best plant choices to attract them include all colors of penta, as well as lantana, plumbago, yarrow, butterfly bush, dill, parsley, clover, dandelions, coleus, zinnia, goldenrod, marigold, wallflowers, alyssum, milkweed, and strong-scented phlox. Interestingly, butterflies don't seem to be too thrilled about roses, especially white varieties.

Butterflies like biodiversity. Your garden doesn't have to have a wild, junky appearance, but it is beneficial to have a broad mix of plant varieties. A pleasant mix of shade trees, understory trees, evergreen and deciduous shrubs, annuals, perennials, and herbs of all kinds is pleasant not only for the butterflies but for you as well. Most butterflies are beneficial in that they feed on pollen and nectar and help to pollinate various flowers. The larvae of butterflies do eat plant foliage but there usually aren't enough of them to do much damage. There are exceptions, however. One of the most serious is the imported cabbageworm. The adult is a beautiful white butterfly. When you see it fluttering around your garden, you'll know that the small green larvae are soon to follow. They are devastating to broccoli, cabbage, kale, and many ornamentals. *Bacillus thuringiensis* (Bt) is the best control for heavy infestations, but beneficial insects such as the trichogramma wasps or other native wasps will help greatly.

Why Feed the Birds?

Several people have asked why I end many of my columns and all my radio shows with the reminder "Don't forget to feed the birds." Others tell me from time to time that I shouldn't feed the birds at all because it makes them lazy. Some even have the nerve to tell me that "it isn't natural."

My recommendation to feed the birds started as an attempt to get people to slow down and take time to enjoy nature. Bird feeding is easy, doesn't take much time, and doesn't cost much. Feeding birds is not harmful to them in any way; it simply supplements their natural diet, as any bird expert will tell you.

Attracting birds to your garden with food or shelter allows you to enjoy their beauty and helps with the control of insects. Purple martins, swifts, and swallows, for example, eat an enormous quantity of flying insects. Hummingbirds also like insects.

Some times of the year are better for bird feeding than others, and birds will appreciate your help more during the winter and summer months. You should feed birds year round but not expect to see as many cardinals, sparrows, doves, and others in the spring, when juicy insects are plentiful and young birds are hungry, or in the fall, when plants are producing plenty of berries and seeds.

Different birds have different feeding habits and are therefore attracted to different foods. Some are almost exclusively seed eaters, while others eat both insects and seeds. Among the seed eaters are cardinals, chickadees, finches, nuthatches, titmice, sparrows, juncoes, jays, doves, pheasant, and quail.

To attract juncoes, doves, and other ground feeders, put oiled sunflower seed and smaller seed on the ground or in dishes. Finches, on the other hand, prefer hanging feeders filled with black thistle seed.

If sprouting occurs under feeders as a result of feeding bird-seed and becomes a nuisance, try using safflower seeds or peanut hearts. These will not germinate under feeders, and birds love them. Many birds love sunflower seeds, but be aware that the hulls are toxic to plants. Expect a dead spot under the feeder, or put the feeder over a paved or mulched area.

Louise Riotte, author of many fine gardening books, suggests planting flowers that produce seeds that birds like, such as coreopsis, cosmos, sunflowers, and verbena. Birds like native grasses such as bluegrasses (*Poa* spp.), grama grasses (*Boutelous* spp.), bluestems (*Andropogon* spp.), wheatgrasses (*Agropyron* spp.), vine mesquite (*Panicum obtusum*), and Indian ricegrass (*Oryzopsis hymenoides*). Other plants or trees that seem to attract birds include hackberry, chokeberry, elderberry, mulberry, dogwood, barberry, Russian olive, yaupon, and hawthorne.

So, whether it's cold and dreary or hot and humid outside, try putting out a little seed to bring nature closer to your home. You can attract birds by feeding them or by giving them habitat. I suggest doing both.

Armadillos, Raccoons, Possums, Squirrels, and Other Critters

Last night I woke up to the sound of little footsteps on the roof. I didn't have to see these visitors to know what they were. Raccoons are frequent uninvited guests to homes and can be very destructive. There are other beasts in this same category. I like animals, but they can be substantial pests. Here are some tips on how to control them The Natural Way.

Raccoons. The best way to control these bandits is to eliminate their food and water sources. Sometimes, however, that's impossible. For instance, I have a fish pond, and there's usually dog food in the bowls in the dog run. It's amazing that raccoons will come to eat dog food even if my dogs are in the run. Several small ones have ended their lives early by underestimating Skeeter and Bo, a pretty good canine tag team. The larger raccoons usually get away, and the dogs usually get a few cuts. Big raccoons can be quite dangerous and can even kill your pets. They also sometimes have rabies, so don't take them lightly. They are smart and extremely dexterous for wild animals; they can open gates, box lids, trash-can covers, and other enclosures.

If dog food is left out at night, raccoons will find it. I noticed that the uneaten dog food left in dishes at night was all gone in the mornings. The water dish gave further proof of raccoons because of floating bits of dog food. I thought I had the solution figured out. I put the large, heavy metal bowl over the small one. It fit snugly against the smooth concrete floor. There was nothing their nimble little fingers could grab, so they'd get frustrated and stop coming in. Wrong! The big dish was flipped over, the dog food gone. My friendly raccoons also ate my Asian pears this year just as they ripened, and in the past, they've eaten my corn as it matured. But I fooled 'em this year—I didn't plant any. For those of you with both corn and raccoons, here are a couple of tips. Hot pepper dusted onto ripening crops repels raccoons and other animals like opossums quite well. On a larger scale, try this: When you plant the corn crop, leave enough room around the outside edge for a band of two or three additional rows. Plant those rows two or three weeks after the first planting. Raccoons will test the ears on the edge of the planting and usually will not go into the middle of the field, where the first crop will ripen and can be harvested earlier than the edge. When the edge plants start to ripen, dust them with hot pepper powder. You may get to eat more corn than the raccoons.

Other repellents that sometimes work include dog droppings, fox urine, human urine, baby powder, snuff, and blood meal. I've had good luck in the vegetable garden this year with a single-wire electrical fence run by a solar-powered control. Putting the wire at about eyeball level works well for coons, possums, cats, and dogs, though it didn't slow the squirrels down at all.

Most animal pests can be caught with live traps, but raccoons are the hardest to catch because they're so smart. Use an unusual bait, something they can't normally get, like sardines, marshmallows, honeyed bread, candy bars, etc., and put a fine wire mesh around the bait part of the trap. Otherwise, they'll just reach in and grab the goodies.

Skunks. Use the same repellent dusts and live-trap method as for raccoons. Skunks are much easier to catch, but handling them after capture is the tricky part. Wear old clothes and goggles, approach the trapped animal with a tarp or heavy blanket, and cover the trap completely. Keep it covered until you release the skunk in the woods. Better still, hire a pest-control company to do it for you.

Opossums. Opossums are really quite interesting animals and not usually a big problem. Try to live with them if you can. If you can't however, these ugly beasts are relatively easy to trap. Here's a homemade trap idea that works well for possums, skunks, and other beasts. Cover a 33-gallon trash can with several layers of newspaper, enough to hold up a bait container of tuna fish, cat food, or other tasty treats. Place a dish of water on the paper next to the bait. Prop a board with cross pieces angled from the top of the can down for easy climbing. The animal will climb up, eat, drink, and slop water out on the paper. Wet paper tears, so the animal falls in, and you cover the top with a tarp or carpet remnant. Transport and release the critter. By the way—don't look into the can if skunks are your problem animal.

That reminds me of a good possum story. A few weeks ago my daughter and I were on the way out to the back garden to gather herbs for bedtime tea. "Gross, Dad—what's that?" exclaimed Logan. It was a small possum under the bird feeder right outside her bedroom window. From the state of it, it was clear that the dogs had been out a few minutes before. It was pretty gory—wet, matted fur, bleeding, grimace with sharp teeth showing—striking! Possum looked real dead. *Oh well, that's life, let's have some tea. I'll put the beast in the compost pile later.* My daughter couldn't wait to show Mom the dead animal. When Judy returned from an appointment, she was pulled into the bedroom to see the messy scene outside—but . . . there was no animal there! Dad and daughter learned the reason for the term "playing possum."

Armadillos. Armadillos aren't too bright and can be caught easily with live traps. To keep these little armored bulldozers from uprooting your garden, set a live trap in the areas where they've been working, and place two boards on edge running out at an angle to form a V with the trap at the point of the V. Use potatoes, carrots, or apples for bait. Although they are not endangered—despite a warning to the contrary that I was recently given by an animal rights advocate—it's still best to take the trapped animal to a wooded area for release.

Squirrels. Of all of the pest questions I get, how to get rid of squirrels is the toughest to answer—with any answer that works, anyway. Short of having a very regular diet of squirrel stew (which is fine by me), I have no foolproof solutions. Red-hot pepper dusted on planting beds or crops sometimes helps. Wire mesh placed on the soil where seeds have been planted keeps the fuzzy-tailed rodents from digging. The bird feeders I've found that keep squirrels out the best are the K-Ultimate, Mandarin, Droll Yankee, and Big Top. Squirrels can be caught with live traps, but there are so many of those little scavengers around that I don't know if that's practical. How do you keep them from eating the pecan crops? Beats me! If you have a good solution, write and let me know. The only thing that sometimes works is to feed them corn in another part of the garden. If they're full of corn, they may not eat as many pecans.

Deer. Deer can be another tough garden pest. Complete control can be achieved only with very tall or electrically powered fences. Various repellents will give some control. Rags soaked in kerosene sometimes help, as do soap, blood meal, and human hair, dog hair, or hair from wild cats put into nylon stockings or fine mesh bags. Other homemade repellents include baby powder, rotten eggs, and hot-pepper powder. Commercial repellents include Hinder and Big Game Repellent.

Using plants that deer don't like can limit your problems.

Deer usually don't like to eat the following: ageratum, ash, black-eyed Susan, black locust, bottle brush, butterfly bush, calla lily, cherry laurel, chives, clematis, columbine, coreopsis, daffodil, daylily, dogwood, dusty miller, elderberry, English ivy, lavender, foxglove, hazelnut, holly, Iceland poppy, iris, jasmine, jonquil, lantana, larkspur, lily, lupine, narcissus, nightshade, oxalis, oleander, pampas grass, peony, persimmon, pine, peppermint, poppy, rosemary, Scotch broom, snowflake, spearmint, spruce, tulip, wax myrtle, yarrow, yucca, and zinnia.

Mice, Rats, Gophers, and Moles

Rodents! While mice are cute and rats are not, both are smart, and both are destructive pests. Exclusion and elimination of food are the first steps in ridding your home of rodents. Sealing up large cracks and holes in the house and garage walls will make it a lot tougher for the beasts to walk right in, and hardware cloth can help to keep rodents from your prized plants. Pet food and bird seed can be tasty attractants for rodents. So can water dishes, food scraps, and food stored in paper and plastic sacks.

Repellents sometimes work beautifully, sometimes not so well. Good choices include tobacco powder (snuff), hot pepper, baby powder, and mustard powder.

To catch rodents, the old-fashioned snap traps are still one of the best choices. Rats and mice tend to stay close to walls for protection, so traps should be placed against walls and in areas where rodents have been seen traveling. Use bacon bits, peanut butter, or cold cuts for bait. It's best to feed them once or twice before loading the traps.

Baits made from Vitamin K inhibitors are the least toxic poisons. These products do not have the worry of secondary kill, as some poisons do. In other words, if your cat eats the dead mouse, the cat won't be poisoned.

Glue-boards are another choice. Smear bulk glue (available from hardware and feed stores) on boards and set them out as traps. Be careful if you have small dogs, and watch out for your lizards, especially the small geckos. When they start getting stuck, it's time to remove the glue and use some other technique.

GOPHERS AND MOLES

In the garden-rodent category, we also have gophers and moles. I have more questions than answers for these little creeps. The good news is that if you have these tunneling rodents, you also have soft, sandy soil. Don't you feel better now?

There are lots of recommended repellents for gophers. They work inconsistently at best, but here they are anyway. Gopher spurge (*Euphorbia lathyrus*) is a fairly dependable repellent. The best way to use the plant is in a solid row planted all along the outside borders of the garden. Other repellents include castor oil and the highly poisonous castor-oil beans, elderberry cuttings, human and dog hair, Juicy Fruit chewing gum, and ferret urine.

Beneficial snakes such as the bull snake and king snake love the taste of gophers, and, no, those snakes won't hurt you. They are totally beneficial.

Flooding sometimes helps, and some gardeners have gone so far as to pipe the exhaust from the lawnmower into the gopher tunnels. Reminds me of Bill Murray and the dancing gopher in *Caddyshack.* Adding hot pepper to the water helps.

Moles are actually not rodents but insectivores. Their primary diet consists of grubs, earthworms, snails, and various other soil animals. They don't eat plants. Their tunnels can be destructive to a vegetable or flower garden, so control is usually necessary. The same repellents mentioned for gophers will sometimes work. The fumigants don't work well on moles because they dig so far everyday. Harpoon-type and other lethal traps are still the most common solution, although there is one electrical device that has shown good promise. It's called Mole Mover II and is available from Gardeners Supply catalog. The solar-cell-powered device rattles every so often and scares the subterranean creatures off to someone else's land.

Predictions

I hope that you have enjoyed my book and that it has helped answer some of your questions on organic gardening. No matter how long the book might have been, I would never have been able to answer every possible question. I've tried to show that there are no hard-and-fast rules and procedures. Organics is about common sense. You can use my experience and advice to provide a starting point, but the final program must be created and managed by the people on the land. Nature is a "whole" and you are part of that whole. Good luck—you're going to enjoy it.

The following trends have begun, and I predict that they will gather steam over the next few years.

1. I predict that more people will be joining the organic ranks. Back in 1988, few organic products other than peat moss and cottonseed meal could be found in nurseries and feed stores. Today, close to half of the gardening-supply stores have a pretty fair selection of organic fertilizers, soil amendments, pest control products, and instructional books. I predict that very soon all nurseries still in business will have substantial organic sections in their stores. Many will go totally organic.

2. I predict that more landscape contractors and lawn-care companies will offer organic services. Many will drop certain of the most troublesome chemicals, such as diazinon, 2,4-D herbicide, and most chemical fungicides. Most companies will add organic techniques such as natural foliar spray programs, soil aeration, and beneficial insect–release programs.

3. I predict that organic food and fiber products will become more available. Small- and large-scale farming operations are already changing toward more sustainable management techniques, and many have discovered that the total organic approach is not only the environmentally correct approach but also the most profitable. Notable producers that have already figured this out include Arrowhead Mills in Hereford, Texas, Fetzer Wines and Gallo Wines in California, Stahmann Pecan Farms in Las Cruces, New Mexico, B3R Country Meats in Childress, Texas,

Crawford Cotton Farms in Muleshoe, Texas, and the Maddox Ranch in Colorado City, Texas.

4. I predict that more and more people will start concentrating on health through nutrition. They will start to apply ancient wisdom and either completely omit white bread, white rice, refined sugar, processed food, preservative-laden foods, and contaminated water from their diet or at least severely limit their intake of these items. Instead, they will choose whole brown rice, whole-grain breads, natural sweeteners, and natural supplements. We will all eat more organically grown food and concentrate on herbs, vegetables, and fruits. More meats will be organically produced from range-fed animals, and they will be eaten in smaller portions. Clean, filtered water will be a high priority, and exercise will become more important—not the strenuous "pump-you-up" stuff, but walking, swimming, gardening, yoga, and other reasonable activities.

5. I predict that quality of life will become a high priority. Home improvement, landscaping, travel to relaxing and beautiful places—probably mostly in this country—will become top goals for American families. Quiet time, reading, and thinking might even become fashionable again.

6. I predict that more public places will ban smoking, that alternative fuels will become more widely available and used, and that recycling will become standard practice for everyone.

Best wishes . . . . and don't forget to feed the birds!

Index

Boldface page numbers indicate detailed discussion of topic.